Forgiveness: The Road to Reconciliation

The Reconciliation Team: (left to right) Tekle Selassie, Molly Rouner, and Arthur Rouner

Forgiveness: The Road to Reconciliation

Arthur A. Rouner, Jr.

Writers Club Press
San Jose New York Lincoln Shanghai

**Forgiveness:
The Road to Reconciliation**

All Rights Reserved © 2002 by Arthur A. Rouner, Jr.

No part of this book may be reproduced or transmitted in any form or by any means, graphic, electronic, or mechanical, including photocopying, recording, taping, or by any information storage retrieval system, without the permission in writing from the publisher.

Writers Club Press
an imprint of iUniverse, Inc.

For information address:
iUniverse, Inc.
5220 S. 16th St., Suite 200
Lincoln, NE 68512
www.iuniverse.com

ISBN: 0-595-23906-4

Printed in the United States of America

Contents

Preface ix
Introduction 1
Chapter 1   The Heart of the Matter 13
Chapter 2   Strangers in a Land of Blood 25
Chapter 3   Making Friends Across the World 33
Chapter 4   The Call to Reconciliation 55
Chapter 5   The Assumptions of Reconciliation 65
Chapter 6   The Work of Healing 77
Chapter 7   Going Gentle into the Land of Genocide ... 85
Chapter 8   The Steps to Reconciliation 93
Chapter 9   The Miracle Process and Power of Prayer .. 105
Chapter 10 New Lives of Mission: "See...I'm Doing a
            New Thing!" 119
About the Author 133

This book is about reconciliation across the world and the longing for forgiveness in every human heart. It is dedicated to all those who love Jesus, who are daily and inevitably "peacemakers" without even knowing it, and who, by their nature, are helpless to do otherwise. May they indeed be blessed, and find that the Kingdom of God is truly theirs.

Preface

After decades of promoting anger as a therapy for freeing oneself to feel better, American society is beginning to explore the possibility that perhaps forgiveness is a more radical and effective way of healing the heart and finding hope for life.

Anger had seemed to fit with our individualistic centering on ourselves. We rehearsed in magazine articles, in sitcoms, in advertising, in counseling sessions, that we should "watch out for Number One," take care of ourselves, and put our own happiness, our own success, or our own feelings, first. We lost the sense of community of putting others first, of caring about the whole.

After decades of a studied self-absorption, what has emerged is a society angry about everything...from the way others drive on the highways, to a lengthening list of what's wrong with our husbands, wives, or children. What is even more dramatic is what we don't like about our fellow students at high school or even grade school. The statistics of divorce and murder on the highway, in the home, and in the school are so horrendous that even therapists who had long promoted the self-subsumed anger process realized that it was not in fact healing people. It had not made them feel better. It was not creating wholeness and certainty, and it was certainly not creating health.

Suddenly there is a new interest in forgiveness as a possible way for people to find freedom, wholeness, and health. A few thoughtful, pioneering books have been written. A national religious journal has done a cover story on "The Forgiveness Factor." A sociologist at the University of Wisconsin has for a decade been studying forgiveness...at first to the dismay of colleagues of the scientific community, but now with intrigued interest. A famous philanthropist is funding explorations of the entire idea of forgiveness.

Such a movement has come perhaps just in time. For in the era of "self," American Christians, even of the evangelical variety, have been so fascinated by positive thinking, successful living, and "name it and claim it" theologies...as well as with evangelism as church growth...and with churches bent on reinventing themselves to be attractive and "user-friendly" to the world, that "repentance" and "confession" have almost dropped from any serious vocabulary of modern day church talk. Even theologians have decried, "Whatever became of *sin*?"

In such an atmosphere, the ancient call of God to the Church to speak prophetically to the world, to call Church and society to humble themselves and to speak, in love, Christ's painful call to the cross...to lives of self-sacrifice and service...had seemed to be largely lost.

Across the world in Rwanda, decades before, the Great East African Revival had been born. As major elements of the Church resisted the influence, being a Christian had become a surface matter, an external identification. It had been easy for the Church to become enchanted with power, with ecclesiastical power and political power. When the government's call to kill had gone out, the Church tragically found itself too close to the government to resist its decree, or to speak to it critically out of the heart of Scripture and the passionate life of Jesus.

Now, however, only forgiveness points any way back toward reconciliation and recovery in that tragically ruptured society.

Rwanda's need and possibility of healing through forgiveness emerges as an unlikely but profound symbol of hope for all places of brokenness across the world. Though it hardly knows how to do so anymore, even America knows that it must turn away from anger, taking the healing road of repentance and confession, and so, to reconciliation.

This book has come out of the experience of a small international team of Christians going to Rwanda and Burundi, trying to help the Christian community of those tiny countries find a way to reconciliation. Its conviction is not only that "reconciliation" is a good thing that is needed in the world, but that it is, in fact, the very first order of business for Christ's Church in the world, and for that reason could well become a whole new name for what a Christian really is…i.e., *Reconciler.*

Introduction

It was very early morning. Only a few vehicles, most of them military or white four-wheel drive United Nations vehicles were slowly moving on the streets below. Our room in one of the few functioning hotels in Kigali, Rwanda, had a small balcony. My wife was standing there, looking out at the morning hills of Rwanda. Mists were rising. The sun had not yet crested "Mille Collines"…the "thousand hills" of this land of forbidding mystery. It recalled the famous anthropologist, Diane Fossey, and her *Gorillas in the Mist*.

My wife stood there a long time. She said nothing, only looked. It was only much later, after our work had began, of leading little healing retreats among the wounded, frightened, and grieving church leaders of that little country trying to recover from the horrors of the genocide, that she told the story of that day.

Though I had been sent into Rwanda with a World Vision leader a year earlier, it was Molly's first time, and her standing there stock still, silently, for so long, was very uncharacteristic. "On that first day," she confessed the next spring to the group of Tutsi and Hutu staff of the Protestant Council of Churches of Rwanda (CPR), who were gathered with us in retreat, "I stared at the beautiful hills of your Rwanda, that had seen such devastating evil in the awful killing time, and I asked God over and over, 'Why have you brought me to this place? I have no skills, no expertise to help these people.' And He had said to me then, and repeatedly in the months that have followed, 'I have brought you here to go to your knees before them, and to ask the forgiveness of these people for what your own people of the West did, to divide them from each other.' And so I want now to kneel here before you to ask your forgiveness for what I and my people did that so hurt and divided you and your people."

With that, she pulled out a chair from that circle of some thirty people, placed it in the center of the room, bowed down, and knelt at the chair, waiting for that stunned circle to come hesitantly. Then one, and then another, began to surround her, laid hands upon her, and prayed for her…the very forgiveness she had asked.

There were many tears. Suddenly Emmanuel, Secretary General of that organization, came forward and said, "If this woman from middle America, with no blood on her hands, can kneel here and ask our forgiveness, then I can do the same." And with that, he too, knelt at the chair, and his colleagues and fellow workers prayed for him.

When he rose there were more tears, and many hugs, and suddenly Emmanuel was telling of his wife and six children fleeing to the church for refuge, and being refused entrance by the priest, and then being cut down by machetes, each one. He then told of his own flight into the forest, of his exile, and of his grief.

Others soon were embracing him, weeping, praying, and confessing their hearts…and even their fear of him. Later came clapping and the dancing, all mingled with tears of joy. One CPR driver said, "I haven't laughed since the genocide." The woman who was his driver said, "He has hardly spoken in three years."

Something strange and wonderful had happened by the power of a Spirit beyond us. A hand of healing had touched that whole company through the means of a simple heartfelt act of confession and repentance. I remember that event vividly because it occurred on my birthday, which the group took time out to celebrate in the midst of the joyful melee of healing and forgiveness. That remarkable phenomenon was repeated many times as my wife has made that simple act part of her witness in the many retreats that have followed, and even in church services large and small.

Something began that spring of 1997, and the winter months leading up to it, that has grown from unlikely beginnings. It has become a movement in the genocide countries of both Rwanda and Burundi.

To friends at home, who in fact first loved, trusted, and supported work we had done at home in communication through television, tapes, and books, through leading "journeys of the heart" to Africa and India, and even to help with famine, water, orphans, and AIDS in Africa, looked at this new twist of ministry into the depth of the human heart so far away, as not only strange, not only improbable, but quite likely impossible. "We thought you were crazy," some of our most faithful friends confessed many months later.

"How could two little old white folks from middle America...even with their Ethiopian colleague, possibly do anything to bring together a bunch of Hutus and Tutsis who were trying to kill each other, ten thousand miles away?" they would ask. They simply couldn't conceive of how it could be done, or what the process could possibly be that would allow us to do anything that could remotely be called "reconciliation."

They thought it presumptuous, if not arrogant. Part of their dismay, we came to realize, was that almost all of these friends...these Christian brothers and sisters...had at least one unreconciled relationship in their lives that they just couldn't seem to overcome. One young businessman said, "Arthur, I understand dams and wells, orphans and AIDS, but I just don't understand 'reconciliation.' But," he went on, "just in case you do learn something about it over there, please let me know. It might help me in my relations with my father!" Because it seemed so hard at home, it looked impossible in far-off, mysterious, and dangerous Africa.

Indeed, the whole process had begun tentatively and in an exploratory and experimental manner. What we knew for sure was that God wanted it, and that He was calling us to undertake it. We knew too, that at least the President of World Vision US, our friend, Dr. Robert Seiple, passionately wanted his organization to be about it...to be doing something to confront and heal the horrible evil which he had personally observed in Rwanda.

What World Vision didn't know, was "How?" There were plenty of ideas of what reconciliation was, and people from the West were already pouring into Rwanda to conduct seminars and workshops on the subject.

But something was wrong. As our team of three went to the African Great Lakes in November of 1996, looking for the answer to "How," one after another…particularly pastors who had attended seminars and workshops and trauma clinics on the subject…protested, "But how can we do all those good things they tell us to do, until we are healed ourselves?"

Suddenly, there it was: The answer. The avenue. The way into the heart of the horror that had been let loose in the soul of Rwanda and Burundi by the calculated, systematic, genocidal killing of April through June of the two years before.

Information about, nor explanation of, the phenomenon was not enough. "How can we function without something happening to us - without some mending of our own broken hearts?"

So, what we *needed* was to find a way for the *experience* of healing to happen. Further, it seemed evident that the target group needed to be the Church…which was so widely expected to be primary agent in the healing of this land…and the Church's leaders, its pastors, women, and youth leaders.

Somehow the method couldn't be preaching. It couldn't be lectures. It wouldn't be for great crowds. It had to be with *individuals*. It had to be listening to the heart…and reaching into the heart. It must make way for God to do what only He can do: The work of Christ the Great Physician.

Somehow we were given the idea of a *retreat* that almost took shape as we began to do it. We felt our way along. We knew we had to sit with the people. There would be no chairs lined up row after row, and no offering of expertise.

"We come as representatives of the World Church," we said, "who care about you. We are not experts. We come to sit with you at the foot of the cross. We come to love, to listen, to just be with you in a circle, ready to follow the Holy Spirit's agenda, to do what we can to open the way for His healing to come and help you to be healed, and to forgive, and so be reconciled."

It began to work. The first retreat was at Scripture Union in Kigali, in late January of 1997. The Evangelical Alliance brought the twelve pastors. One, a busy Baptist minister, was in and out of the retreat, going off to give the opening prayer for the Parliament. Another was the Legal Representative for a Methodist group of churches. James was to become translator and friend, whose church we were to visit, and who now mysteriously just knows when we are in town…and comes "footing" across town to see us.

Gahunga came, young and distracted, clutching to his chest a fancy notebook from some earlier reconciliation seminar he had attended, almost as if to say, "I dare you to tell me anything I haven't heard, to help me in any way." For the first day he sat in a corner and looked at the wall. Yet in the end, when the three days were done, he said, "Something has happened. I am no longer afraid."

Kamanzi was there. He ran the Evangelical Alliance. World Vision had sent him to America to study Peacemaking at Eastern Mennonite University in Virginia, a vital place where much peace work and training is being done for people from all over the world. He had dreams of the country being covered for reconciliation.

Elijah, the denominational executive, deeply feared the Rwandan Church was falling back into its old patterns of being too enchanted with power; that it was too ready to become close…too close…to the government. He was afraid that it was in danger of losing its prophetic place apart.

Mishak, sitting to one side that first day, began to weep…to weep and pray. Finally he said, "I had a vision months ago as I prayed for my country. It was that an Ethiopian would come to help us…and here he is, in our midst." And so he was, our colleague Tekle Selassie, our dear friend of many years, who had come from the World Vision US office after years of being a Country Director in East and South Africa, to be our International Program Director. God had prepared the way in Mishak's heart, and Tekle was a sign.

Later Mishak again wept as if he had made a sudden discovery. "I once was on retreat at Scripture Union and slept in this very room. I remember that I was given a vision of the cross, that we would be led by the cross, and that this cross would somehow draw Rwanda back to God. And now here is the cross, sitting here just six feet from where I lay sleeping those months ago. Surely God is here. He is calling us."

By the time the retreat was ending and we had prayed for seven hours for the group of twelve men, they had grabbed that wooden cross and held it high and were marching around that little room singing and proclaiming that this was the "Kigali" cross, and that there must be one for every city, every region…"until all of Rwanda has come home to Christ."

There was also Pastor Ignace…tall, angular, and bony-cheeked, a little older than the rest. "I had been away in the camps, preaching," he said. "Finally I was able to come home to my village, only to find that many of my extended family had been killed and my own house destroyed. I rented a small house, and moved in with my wife and young child. Then one day I discovered that the man who owned this house I was renting was the very man who had murdered every one of my relatives. And then suddenly, after his death, his family members returned to the town and were homeless. I remembered what Jesus had said, 'If your enemy is hungry, feed him; if he is naked, clothe him.' I did that. I agonized and prayed for two days. Finally, I invited his widow and her children to come and share our rented home. We live there together, to this day, as one family."

Another of the pastors, a Hutu, came to see us the night after the retreat ended. He was hesitant, but put before us his need. He was a new returnee from the camps. His wife and several children were with him. As a Hutu, somewhat suspect in the eyes of the new young Tutsi government, he and all Hutus were forbidden to take jobs for the first six months. They needed to be investigated, to be proven innocent of any previous genocide activity. He was helping as a pastor with a small church, but without pay. Harvest from a small garden was minimal. Could we help?

It was a "Catch-22" which seemed to offer people like him no way to get started. So all of the stories went, of these men who were, through their churches, to be the leaders of the new Rwanda.

The retreat itself was so simple. Twelve people sat in a circle, with a simple wooden cross in the center. We were gathered to be there for three days, with Jesus. The invitation was Jesus' own, given to His disciples: "Come ye apart to a quiet place, and rest awhile."

At a later Rwanda retreat, a young pastor, obviously ill, seemed to be just hanging on. "Why don't you go to your room and lie down," our colleague Tekle suggested to him. We were later to learn that he had malaria. "No!" he insisted. "No one ever before has invited me to have a rest and be with Jesus. I cannot leave!"

We tried to make clear that the invitation was from Jesus and not from us. Participants were to be with Him, for these three days. They accepted it clearly, as just that.

Then they were reminded of Jesus' call to the fisherman by the lake, to follow Him and become "fishers of men." They were invited to walk with Him, to observe, to listen, and to be changed...and so they followed. The retreat attendees did the same.

Then came the discovery and confession of who Jesus was..."The Christ, son of the living God," following Jesus' confidential revelation of the strategy and the direction they would be taking together...a journey to Jerusalem, and to the cross. Despite Peter's protest, they were to go...to see the awful suffering and hear the immortal words from the cross: "Father, forgive them, for they know not what they do."

Those words, we found, became the crucial turning point for most of the nine hundred people in each country who were to go through the retreats in the first five years. "If Jesus, while they were killing Him, would open His arms wide and say, 'Father, forgive them, for they don't even know what they're doing,' then *I can too!*"

It became necessary, in those lands soaked in blood which had been spilled in hatred, to add to the central teaching on the cross, another teaching on "The Meaning of the Blood." The blood of murder can only be cleansed by Jesus' blood which was shed in love.

Central to the retreat was a teaching on forgiveness, and the cost of *un*forgiveness. It seemed important to be factual and matter-of-fact. It was a time to lay before these wounded people a choice. It seemed not a time for sermons. And this led directly to the question: "What pain do you have in your life that you would like to speak of, before the group?"

This invitation has typically led to even six or seven hours of personal, painful stories, which are followed by an individual kneeling before the cross in the center of the room, while the surrounding circle of others lays on hands and prays for the needs expressed.

There is studying the first night, in small groups, of the great "reconciling" passage in *II Corinthians 5:17-21*, with wonderful reports on its meaning given the next day.

The second night they read alone *John 13* and its account of the Last Supper, preparing for the final morning: A teaching on the life and ministry of love…a new way to do ministry, and the picture given of servant ministry…leads to the washing of feet, and the sharing of communion together.

The passing of the peace and singing, following the Lord's Supper, is always a tender time with much hugging and many tears. Sometimes there is an opportunity for those who wish to respond to: "What has it meant to you to spend these three days apart with Jesus?" The most frequent response is that the retreat has been an experience unlike anything they'd had before.

Most of these people have not known each other prior to the retreat, even though these are very small countries. They have not known the pastors or other leaders who have come from other denominations, and they had known people who were of other ethnicities. The retreats are inevitably building bridges across gulfs of broken personal relationships, suspicious ethnic differences, and suspicious denominational differences.

In the first retreat "on the mountain" (at the Jesuit Retreat Center) in Bujumbura, the small retreat group felt they had indeed been on the sacred mountain with Jesus. They did not want to lose the spirit of it, nor the friendships of it.

A gifted young Canadian woman, currently leader of the Mennonite Central Committee in Burundi and Rwanda at that time, had been part of the retreat, and she had helped her comrades find a quiet place where they could meet periodically afterward to pray together, and to share their new friendship with each other, and their deepened friendship with Jesus.

Emmanuel, the young chaplain to the university students, was there, as was the very young Lutheran pastor who had felt so isolated and alone in his work and life before coming to the retreat.

Etienne, at that time head of Scripture Union, was one of the group, as was Sophonie, head of Trans World Radio. Also included was Etienne's pastor, the Legal Representative for his denomination. Not at all sure of us at the beginning, he was eager, when the retreat was over, to invite us to come the next Sunday to give the same message of reconciliation to his church.

And so the work began...with the unlikely team of the white couple from middle America just out of parish ministry, and the Ethiopian refugee from a major NGO, working together, with their own country and cultural differences. They would be taking on this seemingly impossible task...both in the eyes of their friends at home, and quite possibly in the eyes of the World Vision organization that had invited them into partnership for this exact task. Clearly, the impossibility was in the eyes of many of those who came to the retreats.

Two men, a Tutsi and a Hutu, working for one of the evangelical organizations of Rwanda, came to an early retreat held in the town of

Gitarama. They stayed behind afterward to confess, "We came to scoff. What is this Pilgrim Center for Reconciliation? Is this General Motors, or something? Some American organization that has all the answers and will just lecture to us, knowing nothing of our experience? But we stayed, because you are different. You sat in a circle, on our level. You came to love us, and be with us. You didn't have answers. You just cared."

For the first two years we drove the main road between Kigali in Rwanda, and Bujumbura in Burundi. Often we would change vehicles at the border, being met by a World Vision or Africa Revival Minister's vehicle on the other side. The Burundi World Vision vehicle several times flew a white flag to convey to the rebel presence among the mountains that this was an NGO vehicle that came in peace. Curfews in Bujumbura allowed no traffic out of the city before 8:00 AM, or none into the city after 8:00 PM. With the restoration of modest air service, it later seemed the better fact of valor to make that trip by small aircraft.

In extending the work to Burundi we were welcomed in late 1996 by Betty de Jong, Country Director for World Vision. She was the one who opened doors to the Christian community. She enabled us to meet pastors including the young Presbyterian Andre', the former Campus Crusade leader Prosper, and the elegant and humble former foreign Minister of Burundi and once its Ambassador to the United Nations, Ambassador Artemon Simbananiye…who, with his dedicated and effective wife Suzanne, has been critical to the establishment of this approach to ministry in this still fearful and uncertain country.

Betty's own personal experience of retreat enabled her to see early on what the process was making possible. Before she left the country it was she who encouraged us not to give up. "We have tried it all," she said. "This is the one thing that works. It is reaching the heart."

Though we were official partners with World Vision Burundi and World Vision Rwanda, and had been invited there by their own international and US organizations, it was the Africa Revival Ministries

(ARM) organization that we found, in each country, ready to receive and work with us. We learned later that almost mystically, after the tragic loss of three charismatic young founders in a plane crash, ARM was actually waiting for us to come…unbeknownst to them or us…to be their partners. We fell to the work, surrounded by willing and gifted people already sharing a great vision of reconciliation for their countries.

Early on, it was possible, with World Vision's help, to gather in each country, about twenty leaders from across denominational lines, to spend a day in "visioning" the future. We asked the question of them, "How do you see the new Burundi…the new Rwanda?"

It seemed full of presumption on our part, yet respondents came. In Burundi, two Anglican bishops were there or represented. The representative of the Papal Legate, a young Scottish priest fresh from Rome, was there. The head of Catholic Relief Services, the head of World Vision, the head of Trans World Radio, and Legal Representatives from other denominations were there.

Despite skepticism, they resolved to continue. A National Committee for Peace and Reconciliation was formed, with its chair, the Anglican Bishop Bernard. It is for that committee that we work and to which we look for guidance.

Somehow, in God's plan, the cry for help of so many who yearned for the reconciliation of their ethnic groups and their denominations, met the advent and early beginnings of this little team and the retreat model they developed. An ever clearer theology of healing and forgiveness through the process of retreat emerged, and a disciplined yet open series of steps and progress seemed somehow to have been simply given by God. He had created a process that He has been able to use toward healing and true forgiveness that has seemed not of our or anyone's human making. It has been heaven-sent, and miraculous in results.

It is the attempt to lift up and offer the power of reconciliation for the Christian Community, as God's first work for all people and all centuries, that has led us to try to tell the story of the experience we've been given. Further, we offer a new name for Christians…along with "missionaries," "evangelists," "pastors and teachers"…the wonderful name of "Reconcilers."

Arthur A. Rouner, Jr.
Lake Ossipee, New Hampshire

1

The Heart of the Matter

In the painful matter of probing another person's life to get at that person's pain, his burdens, her deep hurt, the heart of the matter is…literally…the heart. In its own way, it is as delicate and difficult as all we might imagine a case of physical heart surgery to be.

The work of the heart…this deep reaching within…is essential if the heart is to be touched, and changed. And it is so much the more if the heart is laden with guilt, walled in by fear, or darkened by the knowledge of what the light would show.

In the gathering of this small room full of strangers who have "come apart to rest awhile," the first step is to invite those present to introduce themselves by telling something of their work and family. This opening time gives everyone an opportunity to decide how much, and how deeply, they want to share.

Our facilitating team begins with an open sharing of their own lives, which acts as an opening door toward a basis of trust between the team members and participants, and the participants with each other. This early time includes a clear statement of our reasons for coming to these countries: That we come to offer ourselves with a word of love from Jesus, the Lord of love, and that we come representing the World Church which has heard of their plight, was moved by it, and cares about them. This is an important factor in countries such as Rwanda and Burundi, where so many individuals express the feeling that they have been forgotten by the world, and by the Church of the world.

During this session some of the participants…often the Hutus…begin to admit their feelings of inferiority and worthlessness.

Scripture, however, reveals that there is no higher and lower, no better and worse, nor no master and slave when it comes to the Kingdom of God, and that we are all of the same blood, and are kin to one another. As a newly-developing group, we are reminded of this:

> "From one man He made every nation of men, that they should inherit the whole earth...In Him we live and move and have our being...We are His offspring."...*Acts 7:26-28*
>
> "Have we not all one Father? Did not one God create us? Why do we profane the covenant of our fathers by breaking the faith with one another?...*Malachi 2:10*

Participants often express visible relief and begin to be at ease when they find we are not bringing gimmicks, and that our guidebook is the *Bible*, and that solutions will only come from God. Noted is the fact that the host organization has taken care to invite leaders to this retreat from different geographic areas who don't know each other that they have attempted to invite a group that includes an equal number of both Hutus and Tutsis, and that the participants cross educational and social lines. In this way, the retreat tends to break down denominational boundaries, becoming a truly ecumenical movement.

Further, the spirit of the retreats is one of "presence"...of people from far away, and perhaps very different from them, who have simply come to be with them. This spirit is lifted up by Edward L. Schmookler in his *Trauma Treatment Manual*:

> "Your presence is the most important gift you can give. Many people think that to help severely emotionally wounded people they should have highly specialized medical training or that they should know the right things to say in order to make them feel better. That is not true. What is most important to badly hurt people is that they know that you are there and that you care. It is often remarkably simple what people need. They need you to be present, focusing your attention on them; and they need you to be open, lis-

tening to them with your heart, and your feelings, feeling with them."...Edward L. Schmookler, *Trauma Treatment Manual*

As Jesus Himself invited his friends to "come to a quiet place apart and rest awhile," the place of retreat is, whenever possible, a room that is simple, fairly quiet, and removed from the mainstream of daily activity. It is offered as a "safe place," with freedom to move about if need be...but of all things, it is *not* a lecture hall.

We also nearly always try to meet in the configuration of a circle, suggesting that we do not come as "experts" having all the answers, who wish to lecture or talk down to them. Rather, we try to come humbly, to be compassionate, to be willing to listen, to share pain, and to come with "empty hands" and open hearts.

Before the cross, societal strata lose significance. The cross is always inside the circle by implication, and one is often physically set upon a table within the center of the circle. It is a simple symbol to embrace, and one readily understood by Christians as symbolic of the price paid for them through the blood of Jesus.

> "For in Him all the fullness of God was pleased to dwell, and through Him, God was pleased to reconcile to Himself all things, whether on earth or in Heaven, by making peace through the blood of His Cross."...*Colossians 1:19-20*

While western society lives to deal in large numbers as a measure of the importance of any gathering...asking such questions as "How many attended?"..."How many were saved?"..."How many were baptized?"...as if these were standards for success, these small retreats work from Jesus' numbers of twelve to fifteen people in each retreat. Such a small group automatically emphasizes and encourages intimacy....As God cares about each of His children...one at a time, so should we.

Further, each person needs time to tell his or her own story. Many retreat participants have endured horrendous experiences, and even after five or six years may never have had anyone in all that time listen to them. Again Edward Schmookler cautions exactly this in his *Trauma Treatment Manual*:

> "Let people tell their story. Generally, people who are healing from horror need to tell their story. They don't need you to push them, but they need to know that you who care are there and want to know and are willing to listen. Being able to re-experience and express these feelings in the context of a trusting relationship can help them to overcome the mistrust, isolation, and damaged relationships that experiencing rape and torture, and witnessing murder, inevitably bring."

Further, from the *Bible*:

> "If we say that we have no sin, we deceive ourselves, and truth is not in us. If we confess our sins, He who is faithful and just will forgive us our sins and cleanse us from all unrighteousness."...*I John I:8-9*

The Pilgrim Center approach encourages each group member to share his or her story, reliving the pain, re-experiencing the guilt of survival or the guilt of inflicting pain or death on another, and allows each to repent of his or her own sins and to ask for, or to grant, forgiveness. All life stories are given as much time as the storyteller needs. As each person is finished, the others share in prayer and laying on of hands for healing the soul.

> "Therefore, confess your sins to one another, and pray for one another, so that you may be healed."...*James 5:16*

Out of the telling of stories comes the possibility of the willingness of each one to go to the center of the circle, kneel down, and receive the laying-on of hands and the spoken aloud healing prayers of this tiny community.

"And this is the confidence that we have in Him, that if we ask anything according to His will, he hears us: And if we know that He hears us, whatsoever we ask, we know that we have the petitions that we desired of Him."...*I John 5:14-15*

"Come to me, all you that are weary and heavy laden, and I will give you rest. Take my yoke upon you, and learn from me; for I am gentle and humble in heart, and you will find rest for your souls."...*Matthew 11:28-29*

Participants are encouraged to forgive, even if the forgiven hasn't asked for forgiveness. Through forgiveness comes freedom for the forgiver, though without confession, the forgiven person remains in bondage. Therefore, a new emphasis on confession by those who are dealing with guilt is encouraged.

The Invitation of the Holy Spirit

Acknowledging the Holy Spirit as the prime actor and means of God's ministry...for speaking to the inner heart of hurt people within the Rwanda/Burundi context...came as an inspiration to our Reconciliation Team. After all, Jesus Himself had said, "I will send the Holy Spirit Who is the Comforter...He will bring all things to your remembrance, whatever I have said unto you."

The Spirit is, supremely, the Comforter. And "comfort," in Latin, means "with strength." So the Spirit is the healer and strength-giver.

Our Team needed, as well, to be in His hands, in these delicate, difficult retreats, and we needed these wounded people...themselves leaders, but now needing to be led by the Good Shepherd, into green pastures of rest and healing...to be in His hands as well.

We felt we could do nothing better than to invite these people to "come apart and rest awhile" as in Jesus' own invitation, and to simply sit "beneath His feet." It was important that the setting be one of the Holy Spirit's creation, and one in which He could work, with the least influence from us.

Therefore, the circular setting said visibly...to the participants' surprise...that this was a company of waiting, with the cross in the center, for the Holy Spirit to lead us. Thus here there would be no elevated platforms, no important people up in front, no podiums, no lectures or lecturers. We would do everything we could to let this be the invitation of the Holy Spirit to come into a setting where the Spirit could lead.

The Advance Preparation of Hearts

Our belief was...and still is...that the Holy Spirit is at work selecting those who will come to these retreats, even before the participants themselves know. Invitations to participate are given by Rwanda and Burundi church leaders. Some of the people invited have wanted to come, and some have not. None of them have known what to expect. Some feared there would be more lectures on reconciliation, which they had already heard many times over.

It was very clear to us that God had already prepared the hearts of all who came...partly by their deep, widespread need, and partly by a strange selecting and choosing process with which we had nothing to do. We just knew that these leaders needed to be received, loved, and treated as "patients"...i.e., people needing *to receive* forgiveness and healing...rather than as "doctors," which had been the way people around them and within their churches had perceived them, and the way in which they had often perceived themselves.

So, their hearts had already been prepared...by Jesus.

Walking on Holy Ground

The bush did not need to burn! In accepting Jesus' invitation to come apart and rest...and simply be "beneath Jesus' feet"...it became almost immediately clear that they were indeed, on "holy ground." The sheer setting aside of time to be apart was for some of them the declaration of holy ground. To some it was the place of the Holy, where the Holy Spirit received them, encountered them, touched them, and mended them. In Bujumbura especially, the participants have referred to the retreat with our team, to our time "on the mountain." The retreat center was located on a mountain overlooking the city, but the retreat itself had also been a "mountaintop experience."

Retreat and rest was high privilege for the participants. Some of the pastors had never had such an experience. Clearly, God came and made the place where they walked holy ground…because it was the place where *He* walked with them.

The Essence

On the second day of the first retreat in Rwanda, in 1997, following a simple teaching on forgiveness and forgiving, an expectant silence fell over the small group of Rwandan pastors as the only woman in the group…a quiet, unassuming Western woman…dropped to her knees in answer to God's calling, and asked for forgiveness on behalf of the whole Western world.

"I ask for your forgiveness and the forgiveness of God for the role our country and the West has played in dividing you from each other," she prayed. Amid tears and unconventional emotion amongst the Rwandan men, the participants offered their forgiveness. A new level of trust, and connectedness to Christ, was born.

That's what reconciliation is about: Repentance and forgiveness, a "revision" of the human soul, a Scripturally-correct transformation of the heart. There is a mystical quality to the work. One learns not to depend on technique or even upon accrued knowledge, but rather on something that *God* does, silently and deeply, through His Spirit working in the human heart in a setting of openness and readiness for Him to work.

The ministry of reconciliation is thus the ministry of new life, of new creation. Sexism, racism, and culture wars are eliminated, not by mere tolerance that leaves people separate, but by the kind of engagement that brings people together. And the source of this creative, reconciling interaction is God: "All this is from God, Who reconciled us to Himself through Christ, and has given us the ministry of reconciliation."

Nothing is more powerful than the words of the participants themselves, who speak from the heart, of their experiences in the genocide, and of what has happened to them in the retreat:

> "My brother was killed in the genocide. I know who killed him. I see him around the town. I hate him. I am tempted to revenge," confessed a youth leader in Burundi early in the retreat. At the end of the retreat, he said, "I can hardly wait to get back home. I am going to seek out my brother's killer and tell him 'I have forgiven you. It is over between us.'"
>
> "We have received a challenge here for each one of us to go out and share with others. The Lord has shown us a way, here at this retreat...I need to pray that there will be a core group raised up to carry this challenge to share the healing messages."
>
> "As you have already seen...there is a problem with the leadership in our society and among the leaders of His Church. We need to be concrete to seek these changes that we have been challenged by God to make in our lives. We could start by visiting each other...our families making exchange visits in our various churches. I think it will be important to meet and spend time with each other to grow a church united for peace in this land."
>
> "With the experiences we have had here, I think God might be training us for the work that is ahead...It is something we can do together...to carry that message of reconciliation through retreat and prayer...God wants to do something new with us now."
>
> "We must be ready for everything. It is lies that corrupted us. Remember these who have come to us from far away, from America, for this retreat. Love pushed them to come. We need this very love."
>
> "We have had many programs since 1993 in this country. But it seems that even the leaders in this country need another help...We have a need for a ministry of reconciliation that will take this word of encouragement to others' hearts. You whom God sent to us, you have responded when others did not."
>
> "I was full of fear...Before coming to this retreat God said to me, 'I am going to do a new thing.' I myself wasn't sure anyone

would come to this retreat, of those I had invited. But the fear is gone...I know that there is something new in my heart

"Yesterday night my brother, Samuel, and I were going to town. For several days now I have been thinking about something very important for our community. I know that many people are for peace, but to this day nobody has been able to raise up a voice stronger than the forces that are tearing us apart. I know that many people pray for peace. But how can we raise one voice for peace? I feel it is unfortunate that our leaders are not more represented here. It is a challenge for each one of us to go out and share that the Lord has shown us a way."

"I can keep on doing what I was doing before. But there is a strength in unity. We need to pray that there will be a core group out of this retreat. Even if it is one small group, as long as we are together, it will be important. You may say that it is like a drop in the ocean, but if I link myself with my sisters, with my brothers...eventually we will be a strong group. We will be able to challenge the other voices. We need to pray each of us to know how the Lord can change Burundi so that it can once more be united in peace."

"As you have already seen from what was reported earlier, the problems in our churches and our society are problems in leadership. The leaders are far from each other. We would like them to come together. I think the healing has started here."

"The Lord uses people who are ready to be used. Thank you [the Pilgrim Center team] for obeying to come to this place. Not many people are coming to Burundi. I had made plans for a crusade with Scripture Union. All the arrangements had been made, and a preacher had been invited to come to lead the event. However, at almost the last moment, that preacher wrote to say that it was too dangerous for him to come to us. And yet, you are here."

"I have had this vision. God has been telling me about responsibility. It's like we have been escaping from our responsibility. Our religion says that we are to count on the Holy Spirit. This is a radical word. But the way we use this word can be for escaping responsibility. We only want to accept responsibility when things are going well. But when things are worse, then we say, 'Lord, it's up to you.'

"But God is saying, 'I have called you and I know you cannot fix things. But with me, I am faithful. I am ready to do the work in you. You need to stand and accept your responsibility.'

"We have been the trouble makers, but since we have been at Jesus' feet…now we are peacemakers. We must accept responsibility. We must be ready for everything. It is love that compels us. Remember those who have come from far away [the Pilgrim Center team] to be with us. Love had pushed them to come. We need this very love.

"With this love Jesus could not escape the Cross. But through the Cross our salvation was there. So now we are responsible. Jesus asked the disciples to come sit at His feet so that they could learn. Then later they were ready to go out. Now we are ready to go out

"First, regarding the leaders in the Church. We are supposed to know our role. We recognize ourselves. We know who we are. But the second part of knowing our role is to have the willingness to take on the tasks of peacemaking.

"We have had programs from 1993 up to this time. But it seems that even the leaders of the country need another help…from the people of God, and especially from the ministers of the Gospel. There is a need for reconciling ministers who are there and ready to lead. Jesus wants His ministers now to perform His work, to take His word of encouragement to the broken-hearted.

"You, whom God sent to us [the Pilgrim Center team], responded. Others did not. I myself called a missionary, 'Why don't you come and be with us awhile?' He responded, 'Brother, you may not come to me and I cannot come to you.' We used to handle our burdens as Christians, by sharing the burden. We would pass it from one to another and thereby we could carry it a long way. We have to be ready to carry the burden when it comes to us. We in Burundi, especially the ministers, must have the willingness to respond to the need and know what the Lord has called us for."

"What will we do with this new thing that we have experienced here? We know that there are many words that destroy…and words can destroy what we have been given. We may not see fruits of this experience tomorrow, but I know that there is something new in my heart: I am a new creature. I am very glad to hear from others that something new is going on. If something new is going on in each one of us here, then I feel we can make a change, we can make a difference. We can be peacemakers."

"I was told of a church where the building had been attacked, and where the cross that hung on the wall had been damaged. The vertical line was still standing, but the cross bar was missing and had been replaced with an AK-47. It seemed to me a symbol of all that is wrong with the Church and society. We want to have the relationship with God, but are unwilling to do the work to have the loving relationships with others at the human level. When I read the Gospels I am constantly amazed to see the ways that Jesus broke down barriers between people…to see how He shows us that we can live with each other."

"The only information we had about this retreat was that there was a team from the US about reconciliation. I wanted to know more. My knowledge of people from America is that they have very big knowledge of how to do things. I expected lectures on strategies, etc.…Western style! When I arrived and opened *II Corinthians 5*, I found nothing new…only a confirmation of my own calling. It was very exciting. I was even more excited to hear that you are not coming to give us things, but to see the will of God coming alive in our lives…When we heard the name 'Pilgrim Center,' I thought, 'Is this General Motors?' But when I come and find a small team of three people, it confirms to me that even one person with Jesus is mighty. It confirms that Jesus and I have the strength for this work of reconciliation."

"This retreat is unique for it creates very close relationship between participants. It is a heart-to-heart ministry in which love and compassion are directly experienced."

"I see that this time apart, it is the answer of God; because this country has had a terrible time of killing and hatred. I myself saw people killing our family. I saw people destroying our house. Now I am going home with forgiveness. I am going home a new creature. As a leader of others, I am going to talk about this reconciliation. There is no more barrier for me…no Tutsi, no Hutu, no Twa."

"I didn't know before how forgiveness can help the offender. Here I have discovered the connection between faith and love.

When you forgive someone for the wrong done to you, you are opening the door so that Christ can come to him [the offender."

"The humility of the Pilgrim Center team expressed by washing our feet is a great lesson for me to serve everyone like Jesus."

And so the stories are told…from different lives, different experiences, and different times of gathering…and yet they are remarkably similar as participants report on being with Jesus in this healing time apart.

For all our team's experience, as we learned and grew, this was the heart of the matter.

2

Strangers in a Land of Blood

Who Dares Go to the Deepest Dark?

There are other parts of our life that are so different from life in Africa.

There is a home in a neighborhood in Edina, Minnesota, where our six children were raised, and where we lived the 32 years of our Colonial Church ministry, and the years since then. Its elm-lined streets would seem full of tradition.

It is a place of privilege. We were called there in 1962 to heal a broken and angry church, divided over a national issue of a denominational merger that sundered many congregations of the free church side of that merger. Colonial was a 1500-member church needing someone to come as a healer…to help the two sides who had fought against each other to come together and go forward.

The tumultuous decade of the 1960's gave us a chance to go into the inner city to serve, and to cross many lines of difference…gradually obscuring the old "merger" walls that had separated Colonial's people from each other. Our task was then to take the wounded suburban church to the real world, beyond the suburb, and show it new ways of serving that could be joyful and fulfilling. And that actually happened. The congregation's arms reached wide, and they became known across two cities for their caring. The church itself grew in numbers, as its own life of prayer and study, fellowship, and worship was growing.

As the young minister's family, we saw ourselves as missionaries. We loved the people God gave us, and tried to serve them selflessly, doing our best to learn, prepare, and offer what we knew in preaching, teaching, healing, and praying, trying to meet every kind of need that seemed to come along. We loved the community, and it was our children's place and ours to live...our home. We tried to be "in the world, but not of it," something our children...and even some parishioners...did not always understand.

Our beloved summer home in Ossipee, New Hampshire, was always a place of physical respite and retreat where, through study, prayer, writing, and climbing mountains with my children, sitting together in the evening to read *The Hobbit,* and *Honest to God,* and to just talk, gave us something of family home life we didn't have in the same way the rest of the year. It was also the place of my upbringing as a child, the "hills of home," where my parents, big sister, and brother lived. It was renewing for the work ahead. I asked the Edina congregation for a study month and a vacation month, to be taken side by side, and promised I would work hard for them in the summer months, and I did that. The time away gave me perspective that I believe helped the thinking, praying, and preaching for their minister when he went back to his people. Ossipee is still part of our life. We are more aware than ever before, of the privilege of that life.

Why then, do we not do what one of the next generation in our family suggested we do: Just forget the world, be glad for our forty years of parish ministry, "rest on our laurels," extend our Ossipee summers, and enjoy the culture of Minnesota winters in the Twin Cities? Why not just stay home?

Why go across the world, almost asking for trouble, to places where we were not known, and not asked by the people to come? Why put our noses into other people's business, particularly when their business was killing, and into experiences of such horrible dimension that we could hardly be expected to understand?

The world, for those four months from April to July of 1994, knew no place of deeper dark. The world recoiled in horror. The pictures...like the starvation pictures from Ethiopia a decade earlier...were in the newspapers and on the television tube for a very short time. Organizations like World Vision told the story and tried to raise money to help. The huge refugee camps just outside Rwanda, caught the world's attention, and when the refugees came streaming back home in their long bedraggled lines, it seemed like a good thing to the world.

So why go there? In fact, who would *dare* to go there? Even after the victory of the Tutsi rebel army and the setting up of a new government, sporadic killing was still happening.

One day, during one of our retreats in Gitarama, an hour or so from Kigali, an ambush assassination occurred only a mile and a half from the retreat center where we were working. The police commandant of that prefecture was stopped and murdered in the main street just outside of town, along with his bodyguard.

Wouldn't golf in Arizona have been better? Wouldn't even quiet writing in New Hampshire be more appropriate to our age and stage? Why would we, of all people, even *dare* to go to such a place and make it our work, our life, our love?

It could only be because God had called us; only because, clearly and compellingly, He *gave* us Rwanda and Burundi, and *sent* us there, as He confirmed, over and over again, by testimony of the people there, that it was the right thing, and that we were even the right people. Why did we go? We *couldn't* refuse to go. It was a call, that's all.

And, the call had been confirmed by the offer of partnership by the huge World Vision organization, asking us to come and "do reconciliation" on their behalf, offering significant funds to help us do the work, and most of all, giving us a member for our staff to lead the new international reconciliation work, one of their finest country directors of Africa, who would lend his fifteen years of experience to walking with us in this uncharted work. Tekle Selassie's very presence, after a friendship with him of many years, was itself a confirmation that this was God's work, and that we...as a little team of three...should not only *dare* to go, but be *glad* to go, and to give God a chance to do what, after all, was *His* work, and not ours.

Who dares, then? We only dare, knowing that we go with angels preparing the way, and that we are both protected and led. It is a joy to do it.

What Have the Most Awful Places to Teach Us?

We go of, course, to serve, to help, and even to teach. But we know we are called to go humbly, to go learning, to go listening…if we are to really help, really to offer something for the peoples' lives, their strength, and their hope.

Such places, with the pain of their wounded people so awful and so obvious before us, teach us above all else, to be humble ourselves. To declare, and make abundantly clear, that we come to follow the Holy Spirit's agenda, that we come to sit in their circle, before the cross, with them. That we come to pray, to love them, to stand with them in their pain and grief, and to offer our comfort, understanding, and faith as we can.

The places of awful pain teach us the depths of evil. They hammer at our theology and cry out to us that no, we cannot be content with the "nice" theological world of much of the mainline American theology that no longer admits of personal evil. We learn that evil is a real force by itself, fired and forged and pumped into the world's atmosphere by a *person*, with a conscious *will* to do evil.

The missionary that *Time* magazine quoted in that awful spring of 1994 may not have been right that "all the world's devils were in Rwanda," but he was right that it was this demon, with his intent to do evil, that had overtaken the heart and spirit of that land. We learn, so naively, and so late, to make a place for real, personal, intentional evil in our world.

Our experience, as we journeyed into those hurt countries, taught us that the devil does not want us there. He attacks our health and our delicate balance as a team together, to try to do us in, to try to defeat us, and to send us away.

But, we also learn the beauty of people. For all their pain, their hurt, their hate…even their guilt, they are the beautiful people. They are the endearing people who live their lives to bring healing, forgiveness, love, and some hope for life, to their land.

And we learn, oddly, that we are safe with them…as safe as we need to be. Plane rides over turbulent Lake Victoria may give pause. Chance crossfire on a street in mid-day we know could happen. Land mines do go off. It could be us in that ambush at any time…caught inadvertently…and it would be over.

So, we learn to trust and know we are in God's hands all the time.

A land mine did go off in February of 1998, just an hour after we had passed that very spot in the road home to Bujumbura from Gitega. We were spared, though a petrol truck was not, and its driver lost his legs in the explosion. We understand that we could have been the ones.

That late winter we were followed to Burundi from Rwanda by another humanitarian team from a large church in Wisconsin. They were on their way to work with our friend, Prosper, for just a week or two, in Burundi. On that uneventful road, about which the US Ambassador to Burundi had warned us, a car ahead was stopped by a group of what appeared to be soldiers. They were ordered out of their vehicle and shot. One soldier waved the vehicle with the Wisconsin reconcilers onward. Their driver floored the accelerator and raced by. They could have been the vehicle stopped. We also could have been stopped, going the other way…even with our World Vision white truce flag flying in the breeze.

We know what could happen. We know too that we have a lifetime of experience. Our children are grown. We're on an assignment from God. We have something to give, and it is now our work.

The Little Team from Middle America

"Who *are* these people, really?" those to whom we go could so easily say. "Jesus we know, and Paul we know, but who are *you*?"

We are a strange trio, that we know. From the American perspective, we are a most unlikely team....but we are perhaps not so strange from Africa's perspective.

For one thing, Africans love old men. They think they know something and that they have wisdom. Though women are valued below cows in some African cultures, the respect for age still holds. A little old white grandmother from Minnesota is enough of an anomaly to be at the very least a respected curiosity. But to learn, as they do, that she and her husband take no salary for coming, earn nothing, and in fact give heavily to the work...and that they leave grandchildren behind...is sobering, and even moving to them.

"You have come so far, at risk to yourselves, leaving so much behind, just to be with us. That is love we do not often see." They soon understand that there is a dynamic of love at work here, and that in itself opens them to our team.

And then there is Tekle, saying, with his wide, crooked smile, "I am an *African*! I am from Ethiopia, but I am an African." He is everywhere, talking with them, helping them, listening to them. He is one of theirs...and, he is a bridge to us...and they accept us.

In our first retreat in Rwanda, one man softly wept in a corner. "I had been asleep once in this very room. I had a dream: that in our need, an Ethiopian would come to help us. And here he is. I can hardly believe it!" God had prepared the way for our little team to be accepted.

Only God could have put us together! Even when Tekle arrived in Minnesota in the fall of 1996, to be the Pilgrim Center's International Program Director, our Center had no plan for Molly to be on our team. She was already busy, traveling to Africa with her own interests in Daystar University.

But Tekle saw the picture and he could declare: "I want Molly on our team." And so she was, balancing the two "boys" and helping it all work. She played a role of wise understanding that led to our greater acceptance in that far-off land.

Clearly, it was the oddity that God used. It was the unlikeliness of this little triumvirate that made it work. It was almost the sense of the ridiculous, the Don Quixote quality of "tilting at windmills" that God seemed to use.

We do come with considerable professional experience. Tekle served 15 years as a country director in Africa for World Vision, after education that includes a master's degree in relief and development. Molly has an undergraduate degree in psychology, with graduate work in education. She has taught in a private school, and has worked in a hospital chaplain's office, and in a sudden infant death center. For four years she managed an international volunteer health organization. I come from forty years of pastoral ministry with an emphasis on bridge-building and reconciliation. My own training goes to the level of a doctoral program in practical ministry.

So, we know something. We are professionals. We have experience…with people, with life, and more than anything, with faith.

We bring ourselves. We come in prayer. We come to love. And the blessings, overwhelming and surprising to us, abound. We are so grateful for this little ministry, with such huge, God-given possibility.

3

Making Friends Across the World

The Call to Africa, Adventure of a Lifetime

I was, as I said, a "country minister," serving almost twenty years a Congregational church, which had grown to about 2,500 members. We knew the challenges of world hunger and had been addressing that as a concern for Christians for several years. We had visited the executive of a major grain company in Minnesota to seek the company's help. They were interested, but wondered how it would be possible to do anything with any hope of making a difference.

I was part of a little early morning gathering of local ministers who led major churches in a suburb of great privilege. The former twenty-year president of Young Life, Dr. Bill Starr, was the convener of this group of busy ministers who sometimes needed persuasion and reminders to be up early and at prayer together those once-a-week early mornings.

Bill Starr had led us repeatedly to and through the great judgment call of Jesus' dividing on His right and left those who had gone to "the least of these my brethren" (*Matthew 25*). It had already stirred us to make a home in our parishes for the wave of refugees coming from Southeast Asia. It had been an exercise in radical prayer.

A dramatic drought and following famine had begun in the early 1980's to reach across the Horn of Africa. Pictures of starving children and great feeding camps began to appear in *Life* magazine and other journals in America. The stories appeared on late night television.

Major world food and relief organizations had begun to move in with help in the form of corn and oil, seeds and blankets.

Then one November Monday in the mid-fall of 1981, two men came knocking at the door of my study in the Colonial Church of Edina, Minnesota. They were from World Vision, the great humanitarian non-governmental organization whose work we had supported for a decade.

"People are dying in the Horn of Africa," they said. "Will you come over and help us? We want you to come to see for yourself, and then raise $250,000 in this affluent suburb to save the lives of these dying people. Already they are gathered in huge feeding camps in Somalia. For many, their cattle have died, and they and their children are beginning to die. They have left their homes and little farms and are on the road, going wherever they hear there is food."

It was a compelling story. It gripped my heart…even as I felt a sinking within me at the thought of even the attempt to raise what seemed to be such a vast amount of money. Yet, when the two men left, I knew that they had delivered a call from God…to my own life, and God willing, to the life of the Colonial Church.

I could have dismissed it as the work of skillful fund-raisers, and left it at that: I could have said nothing. Instead, I fell to my knees and begged God to help me see what this meant, what I was to do, where I was to begin.

I began to tell the story to people in the church, to board people, and to friends. There was remarkable and immediate interest. There was also, by the time it reached the official church council, some opposition. "Why should we feed people who are just going to die six months later, anyway?" said one woman on the council.

Unknown to either of us, the World Vision men had made the same appeal to my Presbyterian colleague across the highway. We determined to take the call to our little group of praying ministerial brothers.

Before that happened, powerful confirming signs appeared. On Thanksgiving Day, I told the story of African hunger to the three congregations that gathered that morning. I showed the picture of the young doctor from Minnesota, standing against a background of what looked like hundreds of little sticks around teepees of a huge Somalian feeding camp. He was holding a little, sick, starving girl in his arms. "This is Dr. Mark Jacobson," I said.

After the middle service a new couple in the church approached me in the line of greeting. "Arthur, we want you to meet Mark Jacobson. He's my brother. He's visiting us for Thanksgiving. He's started a public health degree program at Johns Hopkins."

What could be clearer? One at a time, people came up to me after church to say, "Arthur, this is the right thing. We need to do it. Count on me. I'll go with you. I'll make sure that you are supported to go."

The struggle to make it happen was long and complicated. While some felt some control was slipping away from them, that the church was suddenly moving out not only beyond this suburb, and beyond the inner city of Minneapolis…where we had already been working for two decades…but it was now moving inevitably out beyond Minnesota…to the world. Of course, that was just what was happening, and none of us quite understood the complications and implications of it all.

Strangely, and wonderfully, after meetings and communications and discussions, and praying and planning in five churches, a group of sixteen people…four ministers each with teams of their own people…were boarding a Northwest jet to Chicago, to connect there with KLM for Amsterdam and Nairobi.

It was early February of 1982. Our lives were about to be changed forever. An adventure was opening before us with depths and heights beyond anything we could imagine.

The Building of a Community: The "Africa Group"

In early 1982, World Vision had only once taken anyone to Africa to show them the need and become engaged in the enterprise of caring. Television teams had gone, and one pastor and a business person from Denver had been taken. This was whole new territory...both for World Vision and for us.

Neither they nor we had any idea what was ahead. They had not intended to take sixteen people from five churches to Africa. One pastor or two, and possibly a lay leader or two, was what they had in mind.

Now, "Vision Trips" are a whole part of their work. The taking of church and business people to Africa to see and understand, and come back to tell the story and perhaps to give has now become a ministry, and an important part of their work as an organization.

They were learning, and we were learning, for the first time. The young man who accompanied us became our teacher. He is the one who taught us to pray as we went through customs and airports. He is the one who taught us to watch for angels...to realize that God could be sending people to us to help us, or to direct us...or perhaps to rescue us from complicated, difficult, and even dangerous situations. Some would be visible. Others would be "angels unaware," angels in disguise, people that God gave to us to play the role of angels to help us.

Emerging from Schipol Airport that early gray early morning in 1982, our team of sixteen looked at each other as we headed into Amsterdam and realized we would be together for two weeks...and maybe a lifetime...and we'd better get to know each other.

And so, across the different story lines of five different denominations, as well as our very different personal experiences, we began the long process of building friendships.

We talked about ourselves, our lives, our work, our churches. We talked about Africa and what we knew of the need. We shared some of our fears about what this all could be.

Another long flight took us to Nairobi. From there gradually smaller planes took us north to Lokichar, and finally, across the Cherangari Hills, until finally we were dropping into a dry, red-brown desert land of thorn bushes, and little prickly bushes called "wait a bit," and the world of the Pokot people. A pregnant woman suffering from meningitis was picked up along the road on our long drive from the airstrip at Alale to the "Home of the Little Sheep"...i.e., Kiwawa, Kenya.

A thousand people were lined up at a temporary shelter that had become a feeding place. World Vision had come to supply food for the overwhelmed local missionary to distribute to these quietly starving people. Our first vision of Africa and its need was the long line of people waiting patiently in the noonday sun for a plastic bowl of mush from the big tubs on the low coal fire in the shadowy shelter.

Our team processed these images together, sitting late at night in their Kiwawa house, talking together, listening to missionaries Dick and Jane Hamilton as they told the story of how they came, and who these Pokot people were, what their needs were, and their sense of how much God loved them.

Religiously, they had lived in fear of the various forces that governed their lives. These people had for fifty years resisted efforts to claim them for Christ. But now the famine had changed all that: A few remembered when famine had come once before, in the generation of the grandfathers. People had become so weakened that they were attacked by the hyenas, and had had to seek refuge in caves.

The signs were there again. They were a desperate people. Out in the hills around Kiwawa, perhaps thirty people were dying each day. They knew they could not survive without help. Suddenly, the story of God's own Son Who loved them so much that He gave His life for them seemed plausible, and they were open to that love in a whole new way.

In nearby Nyrapong we saw people so hungry that they could only lie on the ground. A woman in that town approached this strange band of white people, knowing we had come to help. She held up one of her own flattened and empty breasts and repeated pleadingly to one of our now bewildered men. "Miluk, miluk!" She had a child, but no milk with which to feed him.

The one lone Catholic man looked down from his six-foot height with a wretched and helpless look on his face. "I have no milk," he said, and to his teammates he asked, "What can we do?"

We flew by helicopter from Nyrapong, to the little technical school at Kodich, and from there up to the top of Mt. Karakol where we spent the day with people who had just emerged out of the bush when we had arrived. "These mountain people have never seen white people before," our World Vision guide told us. We were overcome by this realization.

We visited the worst of Nairobi's slums, and spent a day out in the Rift Valley with the Masai people. And each day we prayed morning and evening, read Scripture, and talked long into the night...about what this all meant: That such hunger existed in our world. That we could do something. That as people of faith we could not ignore what we had seen and experienced. We began to believe that we could raise the needed money, and that we could give it. We knew that at the very least, we needed to try.

So, we came together: A Catholic layman, a conservative Baptist minister and three men of his church, a Presbyterian minister and three of his people, Bill Starr and two lay Lutherans from his church, and four of us from Colonial, a Congregational church.

True Ecumenism

It had started as a small ministers' prayer group's project, yet now it was much more. It was lay people from each of those ministers' churches seeing the world together, suddenly sharing a whole new experience of life and being shaken by it. They were confronted and rocked by it, being led together by the same Holy Spirit to the deepest human need. We must respond.

We took ourselves very seriously...perhaps much too seriously. Instinctively we felt that we must have a vehicle to describe our life together, through which to do our work and raise funds together. Our vehicle would not be for only one church, but it would be raised in all the churches by all of us...but it had yet to be created.

And so, out of meetings around the pool at Nairobi's Intercontinental Hotel, and then in an Amsterdam Hotel on our sojourn home, the "Christian Volunteers of Minnesota" was formed, with officers, modest by-laws, and very soon, a legal life.

The churches of Edina, Minnesota, with their own theological differences and great contrasts in ministry, Catholic and Protestant, were coming together. We were together...not around theology, liturgy, or mutually shared history, but around a deep and tragic need of the people of the world, forming a new entity in which we all could share...as brothers and sisters across the lines of our many differences.

What was in the making was a true "grass-roots" ecumenism. It would be a coming together of Christians to care, and to take hands with differences seen for what they were...i.e., differences of very little consequence.

The Breaking Down of Local Church Competition and Denominational Walls

The team came back from Africa that first year with Baptists having learned to love Catholics, with Presbyterians contributing their sense of order and organization, with Lutherans exhibiting their characteristic "grace," and somewhat disorganized Congregationalists contributing their Spirit-following pilgrim way that trusted "the sense of the meeting." As we prayed and talked about organization, and Christian Volunteers of Minnesota (CVOM) was born, we found we loved each other. We trusted each other, and we found we could take hands and go forward together.

When we came home, there was the "home team" smiling and cheering with open arms at the head of the gangway at the airport. We sang and prayed thanks.

Mixed teams from all five churches…those who had physically journeyed out and those who had prayed for and supported the travelers…came to each others' churches and stood up during announcements or "concerns" times, and testified to what had happened…in their own hearts.

It was electric. A Spirit moved among the churches. In March, home gatherings for Lenten communion and foot-washing began with slides and the heartfelt story of our CVOM travelers, and of the new, recognizable "Africa Group" within these churches and across our town. A new, true ecumenism began to grow at the very heart of our high-powered town, and among our competitive churches.

God's Leading Hand

It became apparent that another hand than ours was in all of this. On Easter Sunday the five churches out…did the giving asked for by World Vision. The offering raised was not $250,000 but $369,000! The bells all rang. Miracle was in the air.

One resister in the Colonial company, a friend who liked to run things himself, climbed up into the pulpit beside me as the people were coming forward with their offering…the nearly $150,000 that came from Colonial…and said, "Congratulations, Arthur. It was the right thing. You just went about it in the wrong way" (meaning…you should have had us organize it all beforehand, and go through all the boards and groups to give their approval first).

It was so hard for those people to see that God does what He's going to do. He touches. He inspires. He moves. He doesn't always use systems…especially systems that often are used to question and keep things from happening.

It was time to go. The world was starving, and we could help. And our diverse and different churches could agree on hunger, and the need to feed the world. That was the start. That was His timing.

We did not expect the call to come again the next year…but then it came. By 1984, we knew the big feeding camps of Ethiopia. We would soon be going to Alamata, Lalibela, Ibnat, Inde Selassie, and finally to Antsokia.

We were moved very quickly from famine feeding to water resources, wells, dams, capped springs, pumps, and pipes, and then to agriculture, to growing a million seedling trees each year in each of the three experimental farms we were able to help establish on the model of the first, now-famous Antsokia Valley.

So it went on, our calls to church-building, to evangelism, and then…in Uganda…to orphans and AIDS. In Uganda, where President Museveni had come to power by virtually a children's army of orphans, his wife was deeply concerned for them…some orphaned by the war, and some orphaned by the new disease AIDS, that was sweeping Uganda.

As all of these efforts unfolded, at last came the call to the inner heart. Finally, we were made ready to see, and understand the invisible burden of grief…this thing within: so unlike the physical dying of hunger.

It was so unlike building agriculture in the watering of a farm like the veritable Eden that God had fashioned from the death camp of Mekoy, in the Antsokia Valley of Ethiopia. It was even unlike the nurturing and encouraging of new young Christians into becoming elders and leaders of a church…something entirely new to us.

"Why are you doing this…helping us, here in Mekoy?" the young man in the feeding line asked the World Vision worker there at Mekoy's feeding station.

"Because Jesus sent me to do it," was the answer. And so that young man, Demiss, became a believer, and was set aside as an evangelist for the church, which grew and grew.

Then Finally, the Inner Heart

One of our young Minnesota business leaders who has taken back to Africa with him four "Windpump Teams," refers to the idea of his friends accompanying us to help with the work of healing in Rwanda and Burundi, as the "graduate course."

The inner heart is indeed the graduate center of human life and experience. It is that "most deceitful thing" as the *Bible* acknowledges. It is also the place where the great question is answered, "Do you love me, Peter?" and "I demand that you love each other," as Jesus said to His disciples.

Love lives in the heart. When love is betrayed, when trust is ravaged, when friendship sours, or when a bond of human friendship is broken, it is the heart that lies wounded. It is the heart that even physically feels "broken." And when that happens, life itself is imperiled.

When deeds of human destruction are done wantonly across a country, with machetes cutting bodies, splitting skulls and raining bloody death upon neighbors, employees, and anonymous people on lists, the heart of a nation is terrorized. Fear lives everywhere. Every family is affected. No one escapes.

Such psychic, spiritual ravaging is largely inexplicable when its reality is confronted. The hurt is too hard to tell. The terror turns to trauma. Fear marches across the whole land. Recovery seems impossible. Joy seems an experience never to be felt again.

"I have not laughed since the genocide," one excited man said of his experience in one of our earliest retreats.

That is where God has finally taken us…from Kenya's Pokot, our first friends in Africa, to Ethiopia's farmers, to Tanzania's Masai, to South Africa's "Life Beyond Apartheid," to LeSotho's micro-industry, to Uganda's AIDS orphans, and finally to these lands of the broken heart…Rwanda and Burundi.

The Gift of Friends

In all this there came most mysteriously and miraculously, the gift of friends. Many, here in America, wondered how we could be accepted.

"Why would they have you?" they wonder. "What leads them to trust you, to give you even a chance at their lives? You, after all, are white, and old. You represent in many ways, the enemy…the white Colonial powers".

"You must be insane!" some of our best and most supportive friends at least felt, if they did not directly say it. The chance of failure is too great, they feel, as they look at us, and think of the horror these people have been through.

What they do not account for is the power of the heart itself. The heart has positive capacity to open up, receive, and see the center of another's life, to judge goodness, to take the meaning of the spirit and life of another, and to see and hear the heart in it.

Our friends at home, with the most difficulty seeing the point of this work, have gone from incredulity to humbled amazement. Our most Africa-traveled friend confessed much later, "I thought what you were attempting to do was preposterous. But now I see that this work is huge. What God is doing is huge! We need all of us to support it."

Even in Africa, after struggling beginnings in weary, wary Burundi and Rwanda, people have changed their minds overnight.

"When we came yesterday," a Burundi pastor, who had actually helped to plan the retreat, said, "We had many questions about you and your team. But it was all a blessing. We are eager now," he said. "We see you as authentic. You are real. You have touched our hearts. Already you have helped us, blessed us."

Over and over in our retreats we see this kind of change happening in relation to our team. So many have come to Rwanda in the name of reconciliation. Under the rubric of "seminars," instructions are given, theories of trauma are offered, and statistics are preached.

One pastor in Burundi determined he'd had enough. He would not go to another seminar, but he sent his wife and another lay person from his church to a Pilgrim Center retreat. Then, he saw what happened to them. There was a change. He knew he wanted what he now saw in them, whatever it was that was different. He did come, and the theme of reconciliation moved him. Something happened in his own heart. He planned a crusade in his little suburb of Bujumbura. Two thousand people came. Tears flowed and lives changed.

There was something different in what this team from America brought. They did not offer answers. They *sat* with the people. They shared their own struggles. They listened to the hearts of those who came. They reached out to touch them, hold them, pray for them. They lifted up the cross. They taught of forgiveness. They spoke of the life of love, the walk with Jesus. They spoke of servant ministry. They knelt down and washed the feet of those on retreat. They served the Lord's Supper. They believed what they brought. Two of the team came for no pay. They came with love. They offered the cross, and they offered themselves.

Long before that we were on a visit to little Kiwawa, up in northwest Kenya. After a church service in the little church that had had such a painful division for nearly nine years, my African brother Francis…of so many years of service there…said, as the people formed a great greeting circle and said their thanks for the service, "We knew from reading between the lines in the church paper from Colonial, that things have not gone well for you in these last months. But our prayer here in Kiwawa is that God will free you to come here to us."

Francis Kidini has been a friend for almost two decades. So has David Latuu. Many of the young Pokot elders came to Pilgrim Place…our house in their village…as friends. The young elders in Kiwawa became our friends…John and Benjamin and Daniel, who is now the World Vision project manager.

More than a decade ago, the then-Director of World Vision Kenya, said to us through tears, after watching the film, *Out of Africa*, "Arthur, for you and me, it's Out of Africa and into Eternity!"

Even now, years later, those young men of Burundi, working at Youth Ministry in the Africa Renewal Ministry, even asked Molly and me, who are almost three times their age: "Would you be our mentors? Would you meet with us when you come and help us in our faith?" What a compliment to us who in our 70's, are so far from their own age.

So, mysteriously, we have friends across the world. People in northern Ethiopia who know us, have welcomed us many times. Pokot men from little Kiwawa, women in our projects in LeSotho, people of the churches in Nairobi, and in the slums of Mathare Valley know us. They are everywhere, and they have become dear to us.

On every journey out God gives us a very particular blessing to our teams of new and dear friends. Even across the barrier of language came one more whose only communication, besides translation, was body language, and the light in the eye.

"Your pure, clean love touched us," he said. "You offered your embrace. When before, people from the West had only given us the hand."

He had been watching. Between our hearts, something happened.

I think we have needed these friendships. For, strangely, we too, came wounded to their land, to the task of reconciliation. Two of us had been in professional situations of unreconciliation among people who could not bring themselves to be reconciled to us.

In the great Christian development organization where he had served so long, Tekle brought hurt with him. For Molly and me, both colleagues and friends had labored for and allowed our departure from the parish church, while each offer toward steps of reconciliation had been refused. But the gift of healing came to us on the other side of the world...among people for whom we were as different as anything they had known...and they made us friends.

Our team actually have had considerable training by way of background. Tekle has an American Christian College undergraduate degree, a graduate degree in development, and over fifteen years experience in leadership on the African continent with World Vision. He is part of the Ethiopian Church, and he is known throughout much of Africa.

Molly too, has degrees in psychology and teaching. Her leadership experience is quite directly in the area of retreats.

I have degrees, theological study, and years of experience with people in Christian leadership...as well as the spiritual gift of healing.

We are an unlikely team because we are black and white. Because we are American and Ethiopian. Because we are old enough to be in the rocking chair instead of aboard international flights to Kenya, Rwanda, and Burundi. We were not employees of proper, known, international organizations. We were "the odd trio" in our first three years, and it was that dynamic of the unexpected that God used.

Reconciliation Heroes

On the African side, there are already heroes of reconciliation. There are people long since called by God to work in their own countries to bring people together. There are the national heroes who lived through the genocide. They were there. Their own souls have been scarred. Their own lives have been threatened. Their own dear ones have been killed. Their own homes have been invaded by refugees from their own extended families who are now *their* families, *their* charges, *their* responsibilities. Their own salaries are stretched as they try to care for households of twelve and twenty, which would only have been six or eight had it not been for the murder of brothers and sisters whose children are now left to them.

They themselves have had the temptation to "revenge." They have experienced all of the struggles and pain of the dark time.

Antoine Rutasare has been up and down the country preaching the message of reconciliation. From the very days of the genocide in Rwanda, he has told the story of love and forgiveness everywhere...to church workers, pastors, and government people. He has taken the message to the world. He has written and has been widely read.

Antoine is exhausted. He is overworked. His family is overloaded. His financial ends don't meet. He feels a thousand pressures every day.

He is our friend. He has welcomed us. We *work* together.

In Rwanda is also Jean Pierre Kamanzi, former Executive of the Evangelical Alliance of Rwanda. This lanky, lovely man of passionate commitment to Jesus and His reconciling work, has been wherever anything with the name of reconciliation has been going on.

He welcomed everyone who would stand with him in this work. He had seen the bodies and the blood, the buzzards and the battle. He saw Jesus as the answer and he still tells it everywhere. His little house somewhere out of town is his base, and his tiny car…so uncertain…is his means for getting about. Usually he's working several seminars at the same time.

He welcomed us. He saw us off. He planned with us. He is our friend. We have even studied together at Eastern Mennonite University in Virginia, where people who care about reconciliation gather from across the world to learn, grow, and prepare themselves to more deeply understand their difficult work.

In Rwanda there is also Gilbert Habimana…quiet, stolid, ready for anything…leading and developing the work of the Africa Revival Ministries, after its charismatic founder tragically died in a plane crash in Congo on the way to a peace meeting. He puts up with us…particularly with this old white American, with his white hair and his Pokot and Masai bracelets…knowing perfectly well that the Pentecostal constituency, schooled by the missionaries from Sweden of a generation ago, might well be challenged, if not offended. But, he stood by, received us, and helped us through to acceptance.

In Burundi was Gilbert's counterpart and overseer, the young man Samuel Nimubona. Samuel…so daring, welcoming, and believing that God had sent us to help in the work of reconciliation. And so we have been received and given a place, and a chance to do what God has called us to do.

And from that little network others came forward to be our friends. In Bujumbura, Artemon Simbananiye, the "Ambassador" came to see me on the famous front porch of World Vision in the winter of 1995, to talk with me of his dream of a reconciliation center.

Artemon is a real ambassador, having represented his country both in the United Nations and in Ethiopia. He's also served as Burundi's Minister of Foreign Affairs.

His wife, beautiful Suzanne, had prayed for him for ten years, until one day, after a public gathering of many of his peers in government, he knelt down before them and asked Jesus to lead his life. From that moment on, he said, "I will no longer be an ambassador for my country. I am now an Ambassador for Jesus."

The list goes on, too many to name, whom Jesus, in these few years, has given us as dear friends in Christ. They are our colleagues who take us by the hand and show us the way, opening the doors into those places where we can serve.

They are themselves heroes, the modern saints of Africa's Great Lakes...and we, so privileged, work together with them.

What Credibility?

And so we come, ourselves wondering why. Why *would* God choose us, call us, feel He could use us? Why we, among so many? Why we, at this time in our lives?

Credibility is a big issue. In Africa, particularly in these wounded countries of grief, there is great suspicion of do-gooders who come, unbidden from afar, to try to help. The two men who admittedly came to scoff at us in one of our first retreats said later, "We were disarmed by your candor...when you sat in a circle with us and said you were here to seek the Holy Spirit's agency. No one had ever started that way with us before. We stayed because we could see that you had been sent to us, by God."

On our first journey to Rwanda as a team, we stayed in the Diplomate Hotel in Kigali. Molly came to her first great insight standing alone on our little balcony, saying, "O God, what am I doing here? What have I possibly to offer these people, to bring them any word of forgiveness and reconciliation?"

She looked down at the early morning remnants of soldiers in the streets of the quiet city and thought, "I haven't the *right* to tell them anything." And then it came to her: "But I am here on behalf of the One who *can* tell them, and *can* call them to repentance and healing."

Our only credibility is *His* credibility, and such as He gives to us through the friends He offers us, and through, little by little, the work we do, the lives we touch, the burdens the Spirit lifts through us, and the hearts He heals through us.

For sure, the call of the many years in parish ministry was a call to reconciliation. It was a call to build bridges across the chasms dividing people…racially, theologically, economically, denominationally, and socially. So, why *not* now, this call "to the world", and to its darkest places, its most fearful lands, its places of the heart's greatest hurt?

And Tekle, our Ethiopian, our brother…He had chosen to be our friend many years ago, in Africa. He had taught us…in Tanzania and in South Africa. He had patiently spelled it out. He had accepted us. And so friendship had come, deeply in Christ.

He was himself a man without a country, a refugee from the days of the Communist takeover in Ethiopia. Clearly, it was no accident that he would one day come to Minnesota and join hands with us in something to which he and we together were deeply committed, and surely called.

A Center for Reconciliation

And so, our Center came to be…at first two rooms in someone else's office. It was just an address, but it was a place to begin our work.

There had been the "dream team" of friends who worked with us to create the Center's vision in the earliest months before we'd even left the parish church. But soon it was clear that we could not stay in that parish ministry, and that we were being broken out toward something else…toward something that could be much bigger, much wider, and even deeper.

But where? How? Patiently, that team helped Molly and me see what it could be. Philosophies clashed. Other people's dreams and even wounds were thrown into the mixture. And we struggled to see the way.

It would be a "center" for coming together…for planning, for launching. It would be a place from which to "Journey Out" to the world. We took that as a name for our newsletter, now received by nearly 3,000 households. The idea of the "journey" dominated our sense of calling and direction. We were "pilgrims"…on the move, heading out into the world on a great journey.

We would go healing, being a presence in our own city and across the world. We would go to the "wounded healers" of the Church…the ministers left wounded by their churches, their denominations, or even by their families. Quietly and personally, that has been our work.

We've gathered others in early mornings to read the *Bible* and pray. Our volunteers constitute a little fellowship.

Our donors are our "Journey Partners," who give willingly and wonderfully to our work, providing a solid base of perhaps $100,000 annually which helps to keep us "in business." They made possible our salaried part-time staff: Our Executive Director, our Communications Coordinator, and our Reconciliation Assistant.

Of the original 600 donors who generosity made possible a ministry which could succeed the long years of parish ministry, more than half have remained. Others, not even known to us at the beginning, have come along to stand with us. They support us as friends with funds, and in faith as prayer intercessors. As time passed and experience grew, things changed. Doors opened, and suddenly, opportunity knocked.

Our "Niche" Business

Because the World Vision organization had a president who was passionate to do reconciliation work, we were approached…first in 1994, and then in early 1996, to try to help their organization find a way to do it.

No one really knew how to go about it. There were plans and ideas. I was charged to help raise the first $100,000 of a planned $400,000 project that would field a team in Rwanda and Burundi to do such work.

In early winter of 1995, I was sent into Rwanda with World Vision's Swaziland Director, David Montague, to go everywhere, learn all we could, and then go home and tell the story. We were on the way, past $80,000, when it became clear that World Vision's own people in those countries, so deep in the work of relief and development, could not conceive and embrace such an addition. I went to Burundi on my own a year later to help decide the distribution of the funds we had raised.

Then, out of nowhere, came a dream and a plan, that World Vision US and International, would partner with our Center to effect a joint venture in Reconciliation Ministry for the next five years! And so, in the summer of 1996, it happened. Tekle Selassie would come to us. Funds would both come to us and be required of us, and this idea would be given a chance to grow.

As yet, we did not know how to do it. But we went as a team in November of 1996. We asked questions everywhere. Like the Byumba pastors, people everywhere said, "We need you. Please, come. Talk to us. Teach us. Pray with us."

People needed to forgive. They needed to live together or there would be no society. We knew that we ourselves were not going to be able to bring two whole tribes together. Likewise, the government could not be in all those places.

But we soon learned that the Church, despite its failures during the genocide, was desperately needed in those countries. It was there, after all, on the ground, in the villages.

The Church, however, could not lead the communities and the country if it did not find healing itself, or if it did not find its own voice, heart, and spirit again. The Church needed to be healed itself. And how could that happen if the church leaders themselves were not healed?

Many of them voiced it themselves. They had been to every reconciliation seminar they could find. Often the format was of experts coming to lecture them on an understanding of the depth of trauma and how to deal with it. "But," they protested to us, "how can we do all these good things the experts tell us to do, until we are healed ourselves?"

That was the great insight. Our task, we came to believe, was the healing of the leaders, the pastors, youth, and women leaders of the Church. All were hurt. All had lost loved ones. All grieved. Some were even guilty.

These people needed themselves to be healed. They needed to be heard, held, touched, and loved. They needed to be led into wholeness.

We could do that! We could do what Jesus did and call all people apart to be with Him…and there to let Him, through His Holy Spirit, do His own work of healing in them.

And so, the healing retreats began. One after another, the retreats produced the same results: Authentic changing of lives, beginning with the church leaders' own inner healing.

It seemed increasingly clear that our whole work as a Center was really that of "reconciliation"…whether it was out on the American Indian reservations of the Midwest, with ministers and friends around our city, in our cable television weekly program, our daily Faithline phone messages, or our "Journeying Out" with "pilgrim" travelers to Africa and India. Eventually, we were led to change our name, to make it absolutely clear who we were and what we were about: The Pilgrim Center for Reconciliation.

Tekle had come. Our staff had grown. We needed space and just in time, it had come. At a convenient corner in the town where much of our constituency lives we now had our *own* place. Now we could embark into the world of "pay as you go," and always, somehow, it has been possible to cover the rent.

The Slow Acceptance

With all this came the slow reception…at home, in Africa, and even by our partners. Even our best friends felt the call to reconciliation was "too high" and that we could not "attain unto it." Eventually, however, they came to see our small niche, and asked to be a part of it.

In Africa, those who had wondered who we were, soon found out. They learned by the retreats that worked. The Christian leaders who were there told their whole communities what had happened to them, and how they were changed…and who we were.

Slowly, we began to train a few among our African friends to work with us, to stand beside us as our partners there. Others from home have come and learned beside us as well.

Within World Vision there was uncertainty and confusion. Who, after all, were these people, come to do work we ourselves should be able to do? Though they were our partners and had helped to give us life, they initially had trouble understanding. However, they too were persuaded by results, and new understanding grew, and new friends came to be.

Now, we who came as strangers to that land of blood, are seen more and more as brothers and sisters of the same family, ready and able to do the same work, across all lines…because we love the same Lord, Who rules us and has called us all.

4

The Call to Reconciliation

Is It a New Call?

The word "reconciliation" was heard in many quarters in the last days of the 20th century and in the first years of the 21st. Perhaps it is because human hatred, and the feeling and rising rage of anger, seems to have become so common to the American experience, and such a palpable part of the international realities, that the world and its governments have *fear*.

Most countries know about Bosnia and Ireland: People of white skin, the same language but of different faith traditions, who are enraged at each other, remembering generations of hate and injustice. People also think they are right to be "getting back" at those who have, or are perceived to have, hurt them.

Israelis and Palestinians are not very different. Indians and Pakistanis are also equally volatile.

And, gripping the world for a few short months, were also the tiny Central African "Great Lakes" countries of Rwanda and Burundi....These were people of the same color, the same language, and in this case, the same religion, who were so angry, hurt, and suggestible that they killed...even within their own neighborhoods, towns, churches, and families.

The world and its diplomats have *had* to talk of reconciliation. "Can't we just all get along?" was Rodney King of Los Angeles' poignant plea, so apt for our time.

Is it new, this plea for reconciliation? Is it a new movement, some reality of which we just haven't been aware in recent decades?

Curiously, it is God's first work, the first thrust of God's love, His first reach to the world He loved. "God was in Christ reconciling the world to himself." God's purpose was to bring His world and His children home to Him, to break down what St. Paul called "the middle wall of partition."

Forty years of my parish ministry were invested to bring people together: Couples in marriages, children and their parents, inner city with suburbs, white with black, rich with poor, and hurt, disagreeing church folks with each other. But it wasn't called "reconciliation." It was "the right thing to do." It was what communities needed and churches needed, when I started out as a young minister in the mid-1950's.

But suddenly, late in life, as if blinders have come off, life is being seen in a new way! Reconciliation has come, claiming me with a veritable call from God to not only a deeper emphasis and a newly exposed concern, but also a call to *serve*, a work to do, and a place to go.

It is as if God had taken those years of vital, important, valid, and faithful ministry, and used all those years…and all that experience…as preparation for this one strange and difficult task that calls from across the world. It comes so late in life, I can only believe, because it is the world's most important task, God's most critical agenda, and achingly…and with unmistakable clarity…the human race's most desperate need.

It is the most difficult thing I have ever done. It doesn't happen in familiar territory. It isn't doing what seminary or college professors told students to do.

It is work done in a far country, among people of different color, different culture, different experience, and different language from me. And it has taken a lifetime, I believe now, for God to make me ready. At last, in our 70's, God has not only prepared us to do this work full-time, across the world, but He has prepared two of us, as husband and wife, to work together, in this whole new way, in His service.

Rwanda/Burundi: Symbol of the Depths of Evil

People ask: "Why didn't you go to this place or that? Why not work in America...for the inner city...with all its problems?"

The answer is first: "You go where God calls you." He lays His burden on the hearts of those ready to hear it and heed it.

My call to Africa was at the end of 1981. It began with facing the famine in the Horn of Africa, and working to meet that need. Crisis feeding led to involvement with the development of three experimental farms in northern Ethiopia, with agriculture and the growing of millions of seedling trees. That led to capping springs, creating checkdams, drilling wells, and extending pipes in Ethiopia, and building windpumps in northwest Kenya. From there it was help to orphans in Uganda, and to AIDS work in Uganda and Tanzania. And then finally, it led to the unseen burden in the heart...the burden of incalculable grief, guilt, fear and pain in Rwanda and Burundi.

As for America and its needs, the Congregational faith's passion has always been America. It has been to that which its Puritan founders envisioned as "a city set upon a hill, with the eyes of the world upon it." It was God's call to America long ago: To have a humble ministry of serving the world.

We have prayed and worked for the fulfillment of that dream in that spirit, in our apprenticeship for the world, during the twenty years we spent as a large and growing suburban church - building bridges of love and service to the inner city, to Appalachia, and to the Indian reservations of the Dakotas and Minnesota. Other bridges too, were built. It was, in fact, the city and service there that taught us and prepared us for the call to the world.

Perhaps without that long training we would not ourselves have borne the burden of even a look into the depths of evil that had haunted those little countries of the Great Lakes Region of Africa.

The reality of the hate and hurt that had found its way into the heart of Rwanda and Burundi, stands as a sign in the world of the depths of pain and evil that can overtake the human spirit. The results of that spirit that went wild in those lands, seemingly beyond the power of any human reach to contain or control it, stand as a stark sign to the world of what awaits us all if we do not allow the work of love to penetrate our hearts...remaking and transforming our spirits in the interest of hope for human life.

What About Our Need for Reconciliation?

What has confronted and overtaken our theological and spiritual understanding in the process of our study and service in the intense work of the healing retreats we conduct in Central Africa, is that the deepest work of God is what He did on the Cross of Jesus in giving His life for the world. It was love's giving of itself in order to win the world back to the Father from Whom it had turned away. Reconciliation was, from the beginning, the work of calling His children home to Him.

What is seen in such horrible depth in the experience of Rwanda and Burundi, is a picture of what exists deep in the heart of all of us the world over: The capacity, the possibility, of being overtaken by such hate, such hurt, that we...even we...could do what was done there.

Indeed, it is done, we know now, and has been in our century, all around the world: In the death camps of the Nazis, in the gulags of the Soviets, in the killing fields of Cambodia, in the fire-bombings of Belfast, in the "cleansing" actions of Bosnia, and in the suicide bombings of Israel.

And lest we think even those are the only places, we can each one look into our own hearts and acknowledge that most of us have at least one relationship that is unhealed, unreconciled, unmended. We all have hurt, once given, that has not been repaired.

A young businessman, in the same business as his father...though not in the same company...when asked whether he could support our

Ministry of Reconciliation, said: "Arthur, I love you and am glad to support your Center itself, but I cannot support your work of reconciliation in Africa. I understand feeding people who are dying of hunger. I understand dams and wells and windpumps. I understand orphans and AIDS. But I do not understand reconciliation, and how you expect to do it among African tribes so far away. But, just in case you learn something in your work over there, maybe you'd let me know. It might help me in my relationship with my father!"

Because he had a personal relationship, unreconciled in his own heart, he couldn't see how such deep antipathies so far away could be reconciled…especially by us. Most of us are like that young businessman. We have, each of us, our own unresolved relationships which are our daily pain.

We need reconciliation. The world needs reconciliation. It is the very heart of the Gospel's work.

How Hard It is Today to Reconcile

While we speak of fear, hurt, and hate, and of injustices remembered as the things that lead to killing, and the lingering motives that keep us from reconciling, it is *pride* that perhaps most powerfully keeps us from reconciling, and keeps us from going to another with hand held out, taking the immense risk of saying, "Sorry," and trying to build a bridge that you pray God will somehow complete.

"Why," we say, "should I say 'sorry' for something someone else did to me? Why should I put myself down when I am guiltless? Why should I take the blame when it's not my fault?"

That motive, that justification, moves across the world like a sweeping fog of poisonous gas. Every country, every culture, every tribe, every tradition, knows it. Whatever your clan, whatever your culture, whatever your tribe, whatever your color, whatever your tradition…we are the same. Seeking to justify ourselves, we put the blame on someone else for our problems, whatever they may be. "Whoever saves his life shall lose it," Jesus says, "but whoever loses his life for my sake and the Gospel's, shall find it."

Life is given to us when we loosen our grip, cease holding on, and just give it all away. When we have done that with our life, no one can take it away! No one can kill us because we are already dead. We don't *have* to 'get ours'. We don't *have* to defend ourselves. We don't *have* to win. We can listen to others, hear their sides, and see things their way. We can begin to understand and begin to forgive, if we set *ourselves* aside…our lives, our persons, our importance, our dignity, our pride…that keeps us from "humbling ourselves beneath the mighty hand of God" so that He "can raise us up!"

There is something that we didn't *get* that leads us to be angry at the world, and causes us to want to retaliate to get back. There may be some love we feel that didn't come our way when we were children. There may some honor that wasn't given to us for something good we did. Sometimes those we love were assaulted, hurt, lost a job, or were killed, and we feel we must pay back those who did it.

We let ourselves feel cheated. We talk about ourselves, our importance, and our place as we try to win the accolades or make those feel badly who didn't give it back. We all do this in an effort to somehow balance the books or square the ledger. And it never works. We are alone…and a bore…and people see through us and see our pride working overtime.

Nothing works. The wound cuts deeper. The memory only becomes *more* unbearable, and we have too much invested in maintaining our pride, our place, or our blamelessness to be moved by any gesture held out to heal us and the hurt relationship.

American society is full of injustices of wrongs that go unrighted: From slavery never apologized for, from decent education not granted, for people held down by the tragedy of poverty, color of skin, or accent of voice, by clothes, or the look of another land or another culture. And beneath all of these, however tame or violent, stands the issue, the stumbling block, the obstacle of pride.

Reconciling today is breaking down that insidious and powerful barrier. It is so hard for all of us...not the least for our Center's own little team of reconcilers.

You can have pride even in doing the work of reconciliation. Your ego can be built up by the accolades of people who tell you you're doing good because you go to the world to heal it.

But, what about us? We have *our* pride, our egos, too. We want to do well and to tell our story well. We want to do our teaching with a view to be commended and approved, and so to succeed. It's easy to play for this limelight and to let self get in the way...even in the reconciliation business.

The Strugglers are Called

I am not sure that it is only those who have resolved all of life's problems, and who have found "peace, perfect peace," that are the ones called to the ministry of reconciliation.

Among the three who formed the Pilgrim Center Reconciliation Team there was a great deal of very good experience. There were three Bachelor's degrees, three Master's degrees, and a Doctorate degree. There was practical experience in leading country offices for development organizations, coordinating a national office for an international health organization, and heading a large suburban church. There was teaching experience and training experience. All three had had experience leading retreats. We had written books, won prizes, and traveled far before the call ever came to be healers across the world in one of the worst places of pain on earth.

We knew that it was God Who had called. We *knew* He meant us for the work, and for each other.

However, it was only after we were well into it that we did realize this, knowing...as is the case in so many ministries...God uses the hurt and broken to do His work. After attempting to work with a fellow Christian...an attractive, gracious man who had come to do continuing reconciliation work in one of the countries to which we were called, and having one of those unexpected flare-ups human beings too often have, we realized that...at least with this man...God had called three wounded spirits to work together for Him, in the healing work of reconciliation.

Like Charlie Brown, we were tempted to ask, "How could we have problems when we're so nice?" All three men had come earnestly and all meant to do the work to which God had called them. But, where did the tempers come from then, and whence the volatility?

Our friend had had a painful departure from his work in another country. He had done faithful work in a large, much-celebrated Christian service organization. He had come wounded to the place filled with pain. He came with a sense of the injustice done to him. Surely, his heart was crying out about that.

And then, in that far country, he met our man of Africa, a human dynamo full of energy, passion, and faith. But he too, was a man who had been wounded by the very organization he had served so well through all those long fifteen years. He left with little pension, a huge obligation in the house he had bought when he came from Africa, and the sense that good people...his friends...were willing to "hang him out to dry." Though the organization was full of friends, and it was committed to Christ...and he had served them well...his sense of hurt was very great .

And, after 32 years of growing a huge, responsive, and loving congregation, the third one was in the end brought down by friends who wanted a change, and who used diminishment in the form of repeated painful "listening sessions" in which to air their personal pique and petulance. So, grief lingered there too...of rejection, of betrayal, of friends who had turned out to be unfaithful and disloyal.

Possibly the hurt itself was part of our qualification. But clearly, without realizing it, we came wounded to this most important work of our lives.

Forming the Pilgrim Center Reconciliation Team

The Pilgrim Center had existed for two years before the formal Reconciliation Team was formed, and the partnership with World Vision to undertake the work of reconciliation in the Central African countries of the Great Lakes was effected. The Center had grown out of the life and ministry of a large Congregational church in suburban Minnesota, and particularly from my own 32 years of ministry there.

Dear friends had gathered around, wishing that the spirit of the ministry developed in that parish church should not die, but might have a chance to live...possibly in some quite new ways. They gave time, energy, vision, and funds to the enterprise. They, and five to six hundred others, created a corpus of $150,000 to initiate a fund which was at first called The Rouner Center for Missions and Ministry.

Two very small rooms in an office complex, plus a half-time director, a part-time secretary, the unpaid President, and a number of volunteers, was the Center. Television productions, "journeys out," books, teaching, and some preaching and other speaking were our work. And, we went to Africa, accompanying young business men. We had a ministry in town, and to the Midwest Indian Reservations, and to ministers...not a few of them themselves who were "wounded healers." We had always been doing healing work, within the life of the parish, in the city, and even around the world.

World Vision called just after the Rwanda genocide, asking our help to seek funds to mount a World Vision-initiated reconciliation ministry in Rwanda. It was with the Swaziland Director in February of 1995 that I first entered Rwanda. We covered the country, went to Goma and Zaire, walked among the Hutu militia, talked to many of the pastors of Rwanda who were there, and began to understand the wounds and anger of the genocide time. We later did raise funds...about $80,000...and to help dispense them, I returned the next winter to Rwanda and Burundi, where Philippe Guiton, World Vision's Director then, helped me to better understand.

That same winter, World Vision's accompanying guide to our Windpump team acknowledged that World Vision wasn't really doing reconciliation in Africa. "Why not contract it out to the Pilgrim Center to do it for you?" the Windpump leader, Ward Brehm, challenged him. By the time late spring came, that was precisely what World Vision was doing…creating a joint venture partnership that changed our Center's thrust and led the way to a whole new dimension of work.

So it was, by summer's end, that God sent our old friend Tekle Selassie, with long World Vision experience, to join the Center as International Program Director, responsible for leading the way in developing a unique thrust within the Center's work, to undertake…in whatever way God would make possible…a viable way of doing reconciliation in Rwanda and Burundi. Tekle's first act was to say, "I want Molly on our team!" and so she has been, ever since.

Tekle led with contacts and with groundwork. As President, I followed up with letters, helped with plans, raised funds, and went always as part of the team, functioning as its pastor to the people we would gather in retreat.

To have snapped up Molly was a stroke of genius and certainly the Spirit's guidance. It has been a profound call for her, and she has grown stronger every day in our work. Always up to whatever rigors and surprises came along our way, Molly is no longer, as she once said of herself, "a reluctant pilgrim!" She operates under a mighty call and God uses her dramatically and effectively.

Tekle made contacts easily and had powerful instincts for the right thing. Avenues began opening up…far beyond those of our early and logical plans.

I was learning and growing, and leading as I could.

So, the call came, the work has been done, and grows. It is the highest and best, and most important, this little team believes, of anything we have ever done.

5

The Assumptions of Reconciliation

The Original Brokennessv

Reconciliation assumes that something is broken. A relationship is broken, a marriage, a family…even a nation…is somehow broken.

There are feelings. There are memories. There is pain.

The body may appear quite healthy. People and institutions may seem whole, but the heart is hurt. Because words have been said, an injustice took place, or a betrayal happened, everything is changed inside. The mood dwells. The heart broods. The spirit remembers the wrong, the injustice, the betrayal, the awful killing and the rape, the insult, and the injury.

Human life seems never quite to forget that it began broken. The most intimate, most powerful, most valuable relationship of all was broken: The relationship of God's children with their heavenly Father. The very picture in *Genesis* is the story of the original breaking of that deepest tie.

It was rebellion. It was defiance of an ordered life offered by God. It was deliberate disobedience almost for curiosity's sake, but the result was the rupture of the most critical relationship in human life. It was the turning of man's back on God, of defying the parameters God had offered for ordered living. We call it "the Fall," and our experience is that mystically and practically it became the fall of all life from its original harmony and unity with God.

Everything fell. The delicate balance of nature fell, so that earthquake and fire, storm, and wind became possible. The law of tooth and claw turned animals against each other. This original sin of brokenness…in need of being healed…encompassed the entire human race.

Because of the Fall, it seems almost natural that things become broken. A man, long the CEO of the Lenox China Company, was called to head the great relief and development organization, World Vision. Asked about the difference, he said, "At Lenox we had a saying which was a continual reminder whenever anything broke. 'Remember,' they'd always say, 'It's only dishes.' But now it's human life, and that's a very different story."

How Spirits are Broken

For all our psychology and psychoanalyzing, we don't really know how spirits are broken. We suspect that it is by the dashing of dreams…perhaps when an older person does not have a care for a younger person, or perhaps when a child has not been encouraged in the pursuit of those things which come as dreams to many of us. Parents can be too busy; they want children, but then act as if they are a nuisance, or an encumbrance. Attention is lacking. The children's dreams and hopes are unheard.

Something very similar happens in marriages. The blush of the bride is gone. The "bloom is off the rose." Life settles in. The great temptation is to forget the wonder, romance, and adventure of first love. Two people begin to take each other for granted. Little insults hurt each other. Little cruelties are inflicted, the putting down of one by the other. Someday there even comes antipathy: The silent treatment, the grudge held, the offense still remembered…until a hand is lifted, and sometimes even death is done.

Business settings are not very different. Almost always the divisions come over power, over who has it and who wants it. There too, the stampede is on to put someone out and someone else in. Power is the issue…and someone's ego.

Even the Church and the organizations it spawns are places where spirits are broken. After all, the Church is all about the Spirit, and about hurt, lonely spirits who come to church, longing for wholeness. Those vulnerable spirits can all too easily be trampled on by trusted leaders who are not caring, or by Christian friends who turn out to be, after all, as self-centered as the rest of the world. Too often power and competition turn people against each other.

The great reality of life is the fact of its brokenness...its wounds, its remembered slights, and its deep betrayals.

The Cause of Barriers and Breakdowns

The atrocities of the 20th century seem too awful for the human spirit to contemplate. Whether gas chambers, missiles, land mines, snipers' rifles, car bombs, or machetes, these are realities of life that almost no one wants to imagine.

We would just as soon dismiss the users of such instruments as madmen. Normal life seems not to have an explanation. Comfortable Americans have the tenacity to say, of past ages in other lands, "How could they be so cruel...unlike us of the modern day?" or, "How could one tribe turn against another and just kill, kill, kill?" But ask yourself, "What do you think would happen in any American city if AK47's were handed out to disaffected youth between the ages of 13 and 20, as they were in the city of Bujumbura? Do you think we would not have the same killings as they had?"

How self-righteous we can be. How blind we can be to the classic struggles between generations finding their way by testing and rebellion, by struggling for dreams that seem never to be fulfilled.

The struggles of fathers and sons are classic, and sometimes those of mothers and daughters. They are children wanting to be something. And they are parents sometimes fearing for their children, sometimes wanting, ever so much, to guide them.

Everyone is wanting a chance to be someone...to be someone in a family, in a school, in a business, or in a country. We quickly forgive the politician who seems so bent on being in front, being the leader. When he or she wins office, we forgive the chances taken, the corners cut, the underhanded deals made to win that office. We would so rather grant them the mantle of statesmen...of selfless leaders.

Even in churches, the dark hint in the newspapers of some minister strangely being ousted from his or her pulpit, or suddenly resigning without offering any logical or satisfying reason, is usually the iceberg tip of some internal struggle for power. Someone wanted power without understanding what true power is, i.e., the *Spirit's* power in the mystical life of that amazing web of gossamer threads that make up the fragile connection between the dozens, and scores, and hundreds of people who are the body of believers.

Struggles for power in nations often involve the same mistakes and assumptions about what power is, and certainly how you get it, and then, how you exercise it. Politicians run for high office almost never knowing what that life given to others will really cost. Terrible mistakes are made along the way, compromises that change character and break trust...sometimes forever. The barriers are there, and the "middle walls of partition" are built...out of ambition or ego...whatever the rationale or the justification.

A look within even the finest of church communities shows these same temptations to hurt or diminish others for the purpose of gaining power. Cruelties abound wherever human beings give way to the temptation to be self-serving over their bond with their Maker. It is the turning away from God, shown us vividly in the story of the Garden, that is the picture of "the Fall" of us all from the grace we were meant to have...resulting in Classic Sin.

In his book *Reconciliation: Our Greatest Challenge, Our Only Hope,* Curtiss DeYoung lists the "Dividing Walls" as *isolation* and *injustice,* naming sexism, classism, and racism as part of the latter. He further adds *exhaustion* and *betrayal.*

Within the experience of racism in America, he adds *assimilation, tokenism, inferiority, rage* and *fear.* They all bespeak the easy temptation in our human relationships, particularly if we occupy a place of privilege in racial terms.

There are scores of ways of mistreating other human beings. They are designed, consciously or unconsciously, purposefully or not, to hurt, if not kill, another. They are strategies of cruelty, going all the way from indifferent neglect, to passionate, vengeful killing.

The depth of the experience of Rwanda and Burundi in the spring of 1994 was that; whatever had gone before, whatever the injustice and hurts, the remembered grievances, it came to killing…widespread, officially-sanctioned, willful neighborhood, office, street, and even church…killing. The whole land was engulfed in the horror…those who went out, as if on a mission, to kill, and those who lived in fear that they were on the lists of those fingered to *be* killed.

It was a terrible time. To just have been alive while it was happening around you, must have been horrible enough. To then have had your whole family killed before your eyes was triple horror. And then to run for your life into the woods, through the bush, to some hoped for safety, could only have been the most anguished fear.

Those of us who came late to that scene can only imagine what it must have been. To hear the stories and see the lives of those left, and to witness that they are still alive, and even functioning, seems to us testimony to the very power of God, and of the hope He alone gives.

Tribalism…Can We Understand It?

What is tribalism if it is not family feeling in the extreme…if it is not the "Hatfields and McCoys" in their family feuding in America's southern Appalachia, if it is not family loyalty magnified and lifted to the extreme in whatever family or whatever country it is found? We defend our own: Our own children, our own kind, our own blood.

We say it in America, "Blood is thicker than water." Strangely, we are fiercely loyal to our own. Or we should be, as we recoil at the thought of a young mother and father killing their own child because of the baby's inconvenience to them. "How could they?" we ask, because we expect human beings to defend their own.

Does another tribe threaten us with their different color or their different ways? Did the Puerto Ricans not threaten the blacks, when they came into East Harlem, New York, as the blacks had threatened the Italians? Did the Irish not threaten the old Yankees who had only come a few generations earlier than they to New England?

Tribalism, as we look into our own lives and families, would seem to be a vast and intricate network of feelings that have more in the end to do with what power and place that *you*, the newcomer or the favored one, can take away from *me*. It is the degree to which you can diminish me, or even defeat or destroy me.

Surely, it is *fear* of the other that we consider first, instead of considering the marvelous possibility of his cooperation or partnership…his working alongside me that might enhance me and enrich my life, my culture, and even my habits. When those fears are officially adopted by authorities of government or church, and defined and translated into an aggression officially sanctioned and encouraged, tribalism runs wild, as it did in the Great Lakes countries of Central Africa.

Colonial powers early in the century, especially following the great wars of Europe, favored one ethnic group over another. The taller, lighter, pastoral Tutsis were trained and given civil service positions in Rwanda under the colonialism of the French and Belgians.

Quite possibly they thought the Tutsis smarter, whiter, and more like them. In any case, they gave them the upper hand, even though as a tribe they were vastly smaller in numbers than the Hutus. When colonial power withdrew…in this case with little reparation for transition…it was in the hands of the Tutsis that they left the government.

Then when the West demanded democracy as a price for cooperation and help, the majority Hutus voted overwhelmingly for representatives from their own tribe. The Tutsis were out, and it was an opportunity to pay back those who had had power for the abuses they had perpetrated on their subjugated neighbors of the other tribe.

There was the natural temptation that results when vast numbers of people are identified as not only as being different, but as those who had done *hurt*, and even more, as those who might do *future* hurt if they were not stopped right now. Out of this fear came genocide.

What it appears to come down to is the overwhelming sense that "They have hurt me" or, "They *will* hurt me," or, "The deed they have done to me and mine is so horrendous that it is all I can do to keep from taking revenge."

One young man, a sweet boy from all standards we know, is a young Tutsi who had been orphaned by the murder of his parents in an earlier genocide. He was raised as an orphan in neighboring Uganda, under the care of the first lady of Uganda who took many orphans into her care.

After the Tutsi rebel army had gathered in Uganda, moved south, and eventually defeated the Hutu army and government, the way was open for many Tutsi who had left home in earlier days, to now return. Our young friend was among them.

"I came back determined to take revenge for my parents' death. By chance I went to the Youth for Christ retreat that Mr. Tekle led [Tekle Selassie, the Pilgrim Center's International Program Director at the time]. Suddenly, it was as if a stone was lifted from my heart. I was free of that hate, and I did not have to kill."

I later asked him, "But, what were you going to do…search for your parents' killer?"

"Oh, no," he said, "That would be far too hard. I was just going to find two of 'them', and kill them." That a young man so seemingly gentle in spirit could have been ready to do such a thing amazed me, and made it easier to see how soon the impossible becomes possible in the eyes and heart of even the finest, kindest people.

The Great Pauline Assumptions of Reconciliation

The Apostle Paul believed, from his experience, that something happens in the heart of a person when he or she allows Jesus, through His

Spirit, to come in and take over his life. There's a new reality. The hard heart *is* changed. The will *is* redirected. A transformation takes place that has the effect of bringing that person back to God and even back to the human beings from whom He had become alienated.

> "When someone becomes a Christian," Paul writes to the Corinthian Church, "he becomes a brand new person inside. He is not the same any more. A new life has begun. All these new things are from God Who brings us back to Himself through what Christ Jesus did. And God has given us the privilege of urging everyone to come into His favor and be reconciled to him. For, God was in Christ restoring the world to Himself, not counting their sins against them, but blotting them out. This is the wonderful message He has given us to tell others. We are Christ's ambassadors. God is using us to speak to you and we beg you, as though Christ were here, pleading with you to receive the love He offers you.... Be reconciled to God."...*II Corinthians 5:17, Living Bible*

It is overcoming that difference, deeply acknowledged, that Paul names as the very work God was doing, in Christ. It was the work of reconciling His very own to Himself. He was calling home and bringing back His children who had turned away from Him...His children who had "fallen."

It was in receiving Christ that the change could take place in people, and that they could see God and see themselves in a new way, and so, come home to Him, because they themselves had been miraculously changed...as had the young Ugandan when God touched him in retreat.

It is this work of remaking people that was the passion of Paul. His great insight was the significance of Jesus for the life of the world, and the gigantic hope that He, as God's Son, was the bringer of hope for a new world...a redeemed, healed, mended, and united world. To the Roman Church *(Romans 5:6 & 8, Living Bible)*, Paul wrote:

"When we were utterly helpless, with no way of escape, Christ came at just the right time and died for us sinners who had no use for Him. But God showed His great love for us by sending Christ to die for us while we were still sinners."

The depth of our sin, the horror of the evil of which we humans are capable, was very evident to Paul. It is at the heart of the human problem, and precisely this that God addresses in sending His Son to die for us...to make change possible, and to keep sin from being an impassable and impossible barrier, by bringing it down and breaking through it, in order to redeem it. Therefore, the most evil we could ever do could be forgiven, transformed, redeemed.

To the beloved church at Ephesus, Paul underscored the vision of the possibility of new life, reconciliation, and healing, by the work of Christ:

"It is God Himself Who has made us what we are, and gives us new lives from Christ Jesus. And long ages ago He planned that we should spend our lives in helping others."...*Ephesians 2:10, Living Bible*

Here is the plan!...There is a different way for us to live...not by killing and competing, but by serving and helping.

"For Christ Himself is our way of peace. He has made peace between us Jews and you Gentiles by making us all one family, breaking down the wall of contempt that used to separate us. By His death He ended the angry resentment between us...As parts of the same body, our anger against each other has disappeared, for both of us have been reconciled to God. And so the feud ended at last at the Cross." *Ephesians 2:14, 15a, 16, Living Bible*

The anger, the killing instinct, the urge to "revenge" does not need to go on. Peace *is* possible. Healing can happen even between people who have the most horrendous grievances between them.

The Great Jesus Assumptions

Jesus is the very Prince of Peace. "I am come that you might have peace, and have it more abundantly," He promised.

Over and over, it is the same theme: Peace to the inner heart, and reconciliation with God and with each other. Jesus shows us the gathering of a new community...the beloved community of His Body, His family on the earth.

> "I am leaving you with a gift...peace of mind and heart. And the peace I give isn't fragile like the peace the world gives." ...*John 14:27, Living Bible*
>
> "I demand that you love each other as much as I love you..."
>
> "...the greatest love is shown when a person lays down his life for his friends..."
>
> "I demand that you love each other."...*from John 15, Living Bible*

His call to us is to love each other. He offers His own love and says ours is to be like His. "I call you friends," He says.

Even His own hurt relation with the denying Peter was restored through an exercise of love, out by the lake, that wonderful morning after the Resurrection.

"Peter, do you love me...do you love me...are you my friend?"

"Of course," Peter answered. "You already know it. You know I am your friend."

"Then feed my sheep. Take care of my little lambs." Serve. Care for the little ones. Live your love.

Love is the way back. Love is the character of the new life in Christ. Love is the reconciling way.

Reconciliation: The Greatest Theological Truth

It was in Rwanda and Burundi that it became clear to me...after forty years as a parish minister...that the core of the human predicament, the problem of people, and the deep hurt that stops the lives of God's children is the broken relationship…the broken life with God and the broken life with other people; and that the mending of that brokenness is the first purpose of God, the deepest work of the Church. We are to bring people together, home to each other, and home to God.

This is the theological heart of the Good News of God, and therein is the *hope*…the high hope that comes to us in Jesus: The world can be healed.

Genocide is *not* the end. It is not the last word, nor the final reality. The last word is *love*. The high hope is love. The world's future is love. The work of reconciliation is the work of *love*.

6

The Work of Healing

The First Retreat: The Basic Assumption

In our first team journey into Rwanda, we had tried to listen carefully. Stay with us," the Byumba pastors had said. "Talk to us. We are confused. Stay a week, a few days, at least a few hours."

Outside, after the meeting, the translator quoted a fellow Christian as saying, "We are 95% Christian, but how deep?"

Their problem was so like the American Church, like the very thing pollster George Gallup had gradually discovered. Church attendance wasn't nearly the indicator that it should be. There are other factors that tell of deep, immovable commitment. Our friends in Africa sensed that their fellow Rwandan Christians were much like our "Sunday, go to meetin'" Christians.

In meetings in Kigali we heard the longing to go *deep*. The Rwanda Church's crisis had been of its own inner spirit. Somehow, the Great East African Revival, that had begun in Rwanda perhaps forty years before, had not taken root in the Church's soul. A major part of the Church had apparently felt threatened by the revival, and had resisted it.

If we were to help, we had to go to the *depths*. We had to utterly trust God, through His Holy Spirit, to do the work that no amount of organization or lecturing could do. We had to go to the place of tears, the place of confession, the place of repentance. We had to somehow open the doors to that. Further, we had already been told that Rwanda men do not express feelings, and that they are deeply reserved, at least on the outside.

Clearly, lectures would not be enough. Telling them all the answers would not be enough. We would have to trust the Spirit. We would have to depend on prayer. We would have to go back to the experiences, the teachings of the *Bible*, and specifically to the teaching, example, and practices of *Jesus*.

Our basic assumption was purely and simply that He would come. That He would keep His promise, to be in the midst when "two or three gathered together in His Name."

The twelve men who gathered for the first retreat expected lectures. They expected the experts to tell them how to do this difficult work. Instead, the leaders came as friends, brothers and sister, to simply sit with them…in a circle, with no high and no low. There would be no lecterns, no pulpits. We were all on the same level.

Centered in the middle of us was the cross…a physical, wooden cross, before which they were to kneel in prayer. We didn't know that the Pentecostals particularly, had been warned against the cross as a man-made symbol. It was something that Christians didn't need.

Before the retreat was over, they had lifted the cross in their hands, and were marching around the tiny room with it held high above their heads, with all of their hands grasping it. "This is the Kigali Cross. There must be a cross for every prefecture. We will lift it high, and carry it across Rwanda," they cried.

Early in the first retreat one of the twelve men was quietly weeping to one side. Finally he told us his vision of the Ethiopian. Also, he told us of the cross he'd seen standing in the middle of this room. It would be our means of healing, of finding a new direction. "And now it is here. This is a miracle. You have been sent by God. I weep for joy."

The whole second day was given to the pouring out of these men's inner hearts. The hurt…from deep wounds…came pouring out. All we did was give them the opportunity. The Spirit reached within them and undertook the healing work.

Emerging Principles

Even in that first retreat, the principles that would be the vital basis for our work, slowly emerged:

> We were not psychologists.
>
> We were not trauma experts, though we did, collectively, know a great deal about the human heart.
>
> We came independently. We were not World Vision, eventhough we were in partnership. Surprisingly, this was a positive distinction in both countries. Their leaders were very interested in knowing who we were *ourselves*. We came from the World Church…because it cares and we cared.
>
> We came at our own expense, and Molly and I came without salary.
>
> At the first retreat particularly we shared the fact that we had come out of hurt ourselves. We were not as alien to their experience as might appear.
>
> It was probably of some significance that I was a pastor, as were they.
>
> Beyond these principles of identity, there emerged other principles, basic to our work:
>
> We were not coming with our own personal expertise, but were offering concepts and practices that derived solely from Scripture. We were offering, indeed, some of the overlooked principles of the *Bible*. Particularly was this true in the realm of the work of prayer and the practice of the healing ministry. Our teaching and our work with these fellow Christians and fellow pastors was based on ideas they knew perfectly well. We were resorting to the very source and authority they knew best.
>
> One key Biblical principle is that prayer has power. Another is that physical, as well as psychic and spiritual healing regularly results from the earnest and honest offering of prayer.
>
> It became clear that; as the retreat unfolded, they would share in its work:

They would pass back and forth the work of translation.

When one had bared his heart, and come kneeling at the table before the cross, they themselves would do the praying. They would join the retreat team in gathering around, laying on hands, and offering prayer aloud.

We would be growing. Ways of "doing church" would be offered which might be alien to them...not because they weren't in the *Bible*...but because certain of their missionary teachers may have discounted some practices. For example, they were a little nervous at first about foot-washing. Indeed, one of their country's courageous reconciliation leaders was dead set-against the use of foot-washing at a later retreat. "That is not relevant today," he said, with some passion. "That was just for the early Church." Gradually it became evident that this was a vital practice of Jesus, used as a mark of the deepest work, as a sign of servant ministry at the Last Supper, as recorded in *John 13*.

There was an uncertain feeling early on that maybe our work was the mark of some new denomination, or even some new religion, brought by the Pilgrim Center...led by this old man with his white hair, a Cross, and foot washing. The principle of growth emerged as certain profoundly Biblical practices were picked up, used, and incorporated toward healing ends in these retreats.

The Dynamic of Healing

Underlying all the work that we set out to do was the realization that our way of coming at "reconciliation" and attempting to do the work of reconciliation, was not by the social and political means of negotiation, of dividing up interest, of "getting to yes," of "conflict resolution" or of "conflict management." Instead, it was of opening the way for *change* within individuals who were themselves in key places of influence.

Our unique approach was simply to heal the leaders, and specifically the leaders of the Church...the very Church that had been so compromised during the genocide. The Church as a whole had failed to stand against the forces of evil that had overtaken the government and that had called for tribal killing.

It would be a slow process. We would be working with twelve to fifteen people at a time...pastors, women leaders, and youth leaders...and would be investing three days each time with so few people...while an entire country waited. Rwanda had already tried large gatherings for lectures that reached many people at once. "But how can we do that work ourselves until *we* are healed?" was their recurring question.

World Vision's Stan Mooneyham once had asked, "How do you feed a hungry world?" after which he had then answered, "One person at a time."

So far, we see this way as the only sure path of reconciliation...i.e., taking one person at a time into deep personal healing, believing that that one person will then touch his or her church, community, and government.

Our plans in Burundi have been for more and more retreats to be done, led by the pastors and other leaders in their own churches and group. In the meantime, those who had been with us in retreat would not wait. The first little Burundi group talked together about their experience "on the mountain" in a retreat had been held literally on a mountain overlooking Bujumbura.

They agreed to meet regularly to uphold each other. They agreed to set aside a sacred place where they could go for private, personal retreat. But even more, they began to fan out, to spread what they had seen and learned to groups with whom they had some entree.

The executive of TransWorld Radio gathered a group of military leaders of the country for regular Bible study around the theme of reconciliation. He later worked with others who had been in our Gitega retreat to plan a crusade. It was held the following summer in the city square of Gitega, where 10,000 people came. Our colleague Tekle was there and was invited to preach. There were so many people that some were sitting in the trees. Again, the theme was reconciliation. Many were both drawn to Christ and drawn to the call of healed relationships. Gitega itself sits in the heart of the Hutu rebel country and the area of the Twa, the Pygmies, so the crusade was a vital witness.

Others from the first Bujumbura retreat gathered 400 community and country leaders to a gathering in a local hotel. The theme was reconciliation. 125 people made new commitments of their lives.

A cluster of young men, youth leaders in the Africa Revival Ministries, gathered 1,200 to1,400 young people every night for a week-long crusade on reconciliation, touching many lives of young people who had been the killers in the genocide.

Our belief is that healing can happen, and that our task is to open the way so it can.

Why the American Church Fears Healing

The American Church generally has accepted the use of physical medicine and inadvertently allowed its own mandate, its own gift, to pass in favor of surgery, drugs, and the related practices of now "traditional" medicine. It has left its ancient heritage in Jesus' practice of healing to those others who came along and made it central to their work and witness.

The fear of mainline denominational leaders has seemed to be that healing couldn't work, and that if their ministers practiced it, then people would be disappointed, would not be healed, and would, in effect, lose their faith.

The ministry of healing seemed too close to the edge for them. It seemed too dependent on spiritual forces and power rather than on known, universally accepted modern medicine therapies. To that extent they had sold out to the world.

To come at healing today in the mainline, and in even the evangelical churches, elicits fear, trembling, and great humility…as it should. But it is the risk that needs to be taken. a risk that the African Church is much more ready to take. They have watched spiritual forces work.

They have seen healing. Their ideas and assumptions of Biblical healing are not nearly as alien to them.

So in Africa, we have the chance to take this risk.

Rwanda: A Front Line for Learning

The critical work in countries so desperately in need, has an opportunity to run risks and take chances that we would not as likely be allowed to take at home. Where the dark is so deep, and the need is so great, people are more willing to "try anything" in the realm of Christian healing, the dynamics of prayer, the simple truth of human relationships, and in the overwhelming power of love.

Our opportunity is, at this deep level, to learn by experience some of the things that actually work…which otherwise might have seemed too pious, too religious, or too churchy to be taken seriously by American Church people. Even people who know and love us, and who are our friends and supporters, have been skeptical. All of this reconciliation work, done this way, is alien territory to them…even though it is as old as the *Bible.*

Rwanda and Burundi give the Western Church a front line for learning the very things that are most needed by the Western Church. This may well be the unexpected gift that God will give to the World Church…from the hurt and desperate need of His broken and hurt people in the Great Lakes of Central Africa.

7

Going Gentle into the Land of Genocide

One would do well to be very careful upon going into someone else's country. We can tell right away when people from another country are making unwarranted assumptions about our country.

They've missed the subtleties. They've seen phenomena but haven't really understood from whence they came. Frequently they make the wrong assumptions.

One needs to listen a lot, and observe, and hear history, and begin to feel tradition, and sense out of what experience…noble or mean…certain stories, certain prejudices, and certain habits have come.

So, you don't go loud into someone else's country. You don't go brash and bossy. You don't claim center stage.

You go softly. You go unassumingly. You go humbly. And then you hear. You see. You understand what many things mean, and how long it took for them to get that way.

You listen…and only slowly speak…as you seem to gain credibility, and trust.

A Land of Wounded Lives

It is surely the more so going into a land or lands where you know from the news and from history that some one great experience has shaped the lives of many people, and perhaps all people. This is especially so if that great experience is the experience of horror and death...especially death that came violently in the midst of health, and came from the will of others.

What if you enter a country where almost everyone has lost someone to death...and more than that...to murder? You had better not barge in there. You had better not assume they even want you, or that they will think you even dare to care about the heaviest things in those peoples' hearts.

Somehow, to our little team of three, however quixotic we may have appeared to be, and however attempting something that appeared impossible, it was critical that we go with soft steps, a quiet voice, a respectful attitude, and hearts silent until the right time to speak.

We were in a land of wounded lives. We were offering to sit with people who each have terrible hurts in their lives. We were outlanders and invaders, yet they came to us. They took a chance on us. They invested, each of them, three days with us, not knowing how they would be received, or if they would be helped. The leaders of their organizations...themselves taking a chance...had recommended us.

What were these three foreigners about? "Do you come to lecture? To talk at us, and give us all the answers?" Some were surprised to find they could trust us. They were disarmed by our "in-the-circle, before-the-Cross, Spirit-agenda" approach.

Their woundedness, their untold stories of personal hurt and family and community hurt...and surely national hurt...was the crucial center of all the work we could be given to do. That fact had to be uppermost in our minds, and must be the determining factor of what we did, and how we approached these people.

We had to come as their Christian brothers and sister. We had to come with patience. We had to come with both a boldness and an attitude of waitingness because of what had happened at the heart of these little countries, and what was central and formative of their human experiences and their new view of the world.

If your neighbors are a threat to you, if you do not know who may attack you, or who may hold resentment for you, you need to be careful…of whom you trust, of how much you say, of how you relate to others.

Here we are, then, strangers in a land of genocide, trying to hold out the hand of Jesus to these deeply wounded people.

The Compromised Church, the Creative Church

All we knew, as we made our several journeys into Rwanda to learn, to meet people, and to try to explore some way to do reconciliation, was that deep at the center of Rwanda's national life, and high in the experience of many people's individual lives, was that something had happened to the Church.

The Church had faced a supreme test; and, as a whole, had been found wanting. The Church in that land encompassed probably 90% of the people in some way or another. The Church was there, in its Roman Catholic form, its Pentecostal form, its Anglican, Baptist, Presbyterian and other Protestant forms, and had had the chance to play some role.

Prior to the genocide, fears were mounting. Government spokesmen were whipping up feelings almost to a frenzy. Every technique of propaganda was being used…in a country in which as many as 60% of the people were illiterate, and where most of the people lived a fragile existence in an economy dependent on the simplest forms of agriculture and husbandry.

For at least two generations, within the life of the 20th century, there had come a history of fear and tension between the two major ethnic groups…fear and favoritism fostered in too many instances by colonial powers from the West. The tribes had been played off against each other, creating fear by one tribe toward the other. The idea that the other group might hurt you was not at all without foundation, and government leaders, in their own fear, played upon this.

A rebel force had gathered to the north, and had begun to move south. As the threatened Hutu government began to realize they were going to lose, the whole strange process of the genocide began to unfold, with the word going out that Tutsis and moderate Hutus must be killed.

Yet, they were fellow-townsmen. They were fellow churchmen. They were friends. They were neighbors. Militia came into neighborhoods with lists of those who were to be killed. People saw their family members killed before their eyes. All stood to lose their own lives.

Where in all this would the Church stand? Who could rise up and decry the killing, and defy the government in spoken word and personal action? Which pastors and priests would say, "No more!"?

Who knows, in any land, what we who are leaders of the Church would have done? Who among us dares to say we would have stood up and said, "Here I stand. I can do no other. God help me."

We know that some leaders did exactly that, and they paid with their lives. Some fled the field in order to live to fight another day. Some were so hopelessly entwined with the structures of power and relationships with government and government people that they could not remove themselves, and sought ways to support the government, and make common cause with the government, and even aid and abet the government.

Some secretly gave names to the government of people to eliminate. Some cooperated and even took leadership in the spying, killing work of the civilian Interhamwe. A few led killers to their churches, where parishioners had been gathered for safety, and went out by another door, leaving their own people to be massacred. And probably no one knows how many pastors actually raised their hands and struck down people who were their own charges before God.

Fear gripped the country and gripped the Church. At least the perception of the people was that the Church with all its power and influence, with its congregations large and small, in every city and town, did not stand against the killing work of the genocide. The Church did not go to the barricades. It did not go to the cross.

The Church is now under a new government that desperately needs the Church to regain its standing with the people, and needs it to give moral as well as spiritual leadership to both congregation and townspeople. It is there, in every village and town, often with new pastors who have come in since the genocide...from Uganda, Zaire, or Tanzania. It is struggling to regain trust with the people, and is eager to give leadership. Yet it is uncertain, and in many ways confused, bearing the burden of the earlier compromise, and it is still surrounded by fear, and still bearing...in the case of all the Church's leaders...their own pain, grief, guilt, and fear.

Tentative Leaders, Longing to Lead

Hear are "wounded healers" earnestly longing to do what God needs them to do, and already what the young government needs them to do. However, by their own admission, they themselves are unhealed. They came to our little retreats needing something for *themselves*...something that must happen to *them*, in *their* inner hearts, before they could step out and bravely give their congregations and their communities the forceful, faithful leadership they need.

Much of the leadership of the Church and church organizations were themselves of the majority Hutu population. With the confusion and fear of the genocide, many of them fled. The present leaders of the Church and its organizations are for the most part new leaders who come to their positions as Tutsis. Some were not even in the country at the time of the killing, but have come back to serve when they felt safe to come.

For many, there were family members in Rwanda who were killed. Some have come back to find all family gone. They want to lead. They long to serve. They believe Christ has called them to this task. But they too, grieve. They too, lost loved ones. They too, suffered...whether outside or in. A deep work needs to take place in these men's lives. They need to forgive. They need to have their own pain healed.

One of the pastors in our first retreat, a Tutsi, had been away in Tanzania as a result of the genocide. He had preached and tried to help others of his refugee population in Tanzania. When he came back to his home village in Rwanda, he found his entire extended family had been killed. He rented a home.

He discovered in time that the person who had murdered his family had been the owner of the house he was in. Soon that man's family came back from exile. They had no place to live. He invited that family to live with him, as one family. Such great forgiveness had taken place.

Yet he continued to feel fear. He preached in many churches but when invited to stay after for a meal, he always refused. "I am fasting," he would say. Actually, he said, "I was afraid they might poison me."

Upon our return several months later, he said, "Something has changed. I am not afraid anymore." The chance to lead does not come easily. The lessons of reconciliation and healing often come very slowly.

Going in the Spirity

It is to people who have been through such things that we go…to people who have walked through such depths.

It was given us at the very beginning that we needed to go to our healing retreat work "in the Spirit." We needed to go utterly dependent upon God and His Spirit, and not at all as experts who have an answer…particularly the good, helpful, human, but secular answers that come out of all the reasoned approaches from trauma theory and psychological understanding.

Somehow we knew that if we went with the answers, we would fail. We did not have the answers. We found after awhile it was important for us to confess that right at the beginning.

We made it very clear in each of our retreats that we believed the agenda would be the Spirit's agenda. That while we were prepared, we were there with them to be led together by the Holy Spirit in what He would do with us all.

We did not come to lecture. We did not come to stand above them as experts. We came to learn…to learn especially from the Spirit, but very much from all of them…out of their experience.

The People Were Our Teachers

Their own stories humbled us and guided us. We learned their history, and realized that their divisions were as much thrust upon them by the colonial powers of the West, as by any innate difference of their own. It became very important for us to make it clear that we repented of that and sought their forgiveness. Molly led us all in that. She went to her knees before the Cross, making that confession and specifically asking their forgiveness for her.

8

The Steps to Reconciliation

Who knows what the steps to reconciliation really are? Who knows how the human heart is touched in its deepest places, and how its wounds are really healed, and its spirit set free to live again. Most of all, who knows how it happens that a person can be at one with those people against whom a great barrier had been built?

Many came eagerly to Rwanda and Burundi to help, and their approaches have helped in the overall healing work. A gifted, humble young leader of one of the great revival ministries in Rwanda commented on these good efforts in a letter to our Center:

> "So much effort has been made to help our country turn on the way of healing and reconciliation. Many have come using many approaches and models. Some are psychology or psychiatry based. Some have big manuals and instruction books. I personally believe that God uses every effort in one way or another. However, the approach God has led you to follow has been a special gift not only for me but for all of us who have in the past participated in the Pilgrim Center healing and reconciliation retreat. I appreciate the following characteristics:
> 1. Simplicity and transferability
> 2. Relevant and unintimidating
> 3. Rooted on (in) what our people know…the *Bible*
> 4. Understandable and sustainable
> 5. Speaking to and dealing with the heart"

So, our Center went too, to Rwanda, seeking to find the ways that we could help…and particularly seeking the ways that God might use our peculiar little team.

"Come Apart and Rest Awhile"

The work began, strangely, with a theological concept of rest. In one retreat with many Pentecostal pastors in Gitarama, outside of Kigali, a young man appeared to be ill. Our Tekle talked and prayed with him. "You have malaria," Tekle said. "I urge you to go to your room and just rest."

"No," he answered. "I'm staying right here, even if I have to lie down. In all my ministry, no one has even invited me to come and be with Jesus and just rest in Him. I need this. I'm staying."

Something surprising was already taking place. We came to realize that in the African Church there is little concept, especially among church leaders, of rest, of "Sabbath," of a day off, of going apart alone.

Christianity is growing on the African continent, some have said by as many as 17,000 people a day. Molly and I had found that the pastors we had taught earlier at Daystar University in Nairobi had people lined up outside their door at 7:00 in the morning, seeking counsel or physical help. These men were doing their ministry without the aid of telephone or car. And they were daily overwhelmed with people's needs. There was little time left for study or prayer. On Sunday it was tempting to offer loudness as evidence of "the anointing," sometimes on a basis of not much study. The sheer human need kept God's servants from the kind of rest they most needed.

On our little retreats the pastors were immediately taken by surprise. "Jesus calls you to come away with Him, to come and rest," was our first approach to them.

Many of them had been to other reconciliation meetings. Most of them, whether done by their own Rwandan leaders or by good-hearted white westerners, tended to offer lectures or sermons, as a way of telling people they needed to be reconciled. They were told why. In seminars they were given theories on what has happened to people, the psychology of trauma, what has happened to the human mind...and indeed, what needs to happen.

So, they were already a little surprised to find that as they came, somewhat apprehensively...if not suspiciously...to our retreat, there was no lecture, no podium, no lectern and blackboard up front, nor any huge trauma notebook or list of expectations on a blackboard. "We will sit in a circle before the cross, at the feet of Jesus," was essentially the introduction and invitation they received, as they gathered with us in the small room of our admittedly low-budget retreat.

It was intriguing, new, and in the end exciting to them, to be invited by Jesus to simply "rest." To just be with Him. To just be open to allow Him, through His Spirit, to work with and within them.

While there would be some teaching, the mode was by *participation*...by being together, on the same level, and learning...without the lecture emphasis of notebooks and note-taking. They were just to *be*.

Being with Jesus

Our emphasis, we discovered, needed to be on Jesus personally. It must not be on "The Christ," as liberal churchmen in America love to describe Him, keeping Him institutional, theological, at arm's length, the One who fills a certain role. Rather, our emphasis needed to be what we believe the whole Church needs Him to be...i.e., Jesus the *Person*, the God-Man, if you will. He must be the One who "walks with us, and talks with us, and tells us we are His own!"

The Christians of Africa are very used to dealing with spiritual reality. They know about "the spirits," especially the evil spirits. So it is not strange for them to think of Jesus coming to them...personally and presently...in His Holy Spirit, to be with them.

The marvel is that He would...particularly to *them*, who, in their country lives and their church lives, and maybe in their personal lives, have grieved Him so. To be received and invited into His presence...by Jesus Himself...is overwhelming and wonderful to them. It bears immediately the promise, the possibility, and surely the hope, of forgiveness, and of their own healing.

The invitation, then, is exciting in itself. The offer is made of a journey...a kind of pilgrimage...very like the journey on which Jesus invited each of the disciples, beginning with those two sets of fishermen down by the beach in Galilee.

In fact, that is the case made to them...that the open-ended "journey with Jesus" into which they are being invited that afternoon in Rwanda or Burundi, is exactly the journey on which Jesus' first disciples were invited. They too, so long ago, were an unknown quantity. They too, were untested. Jesus took them "right where they were" to follow Him, come with Him, and become something different. They too had been invited to learn by doing, by walking the trail with Jesus, by watching Him work, listening to Him teach, and seeing before their eyes what God was doing in and through this man. They saw how God works!

They could look into the firelight of the camp at night and hear Jesus' messages, His sudden insights, His wonderful stories told as parables. They would catch His character.

It was another way of learning, and we know today it is great teaching. It was open-ended. It was gentle. It took account of the listeners...telling the truth *this* way and then *that* way...and repeating if need be. It would be respectful, quiet, and determined.

It would be a *pilgrim journey*. A walk with the Master. It would be, literally, a traveling seminar, and Jesus was inviting them, in this day, into exactly the same process with Him.

It would be learning by presence and being in His company. We reassured them that Jesus did not show up at the beach, gather the fisherman around and say, "Hello boys, you look like lads of high potential. Here's a theological text I'd like you to study. Read it over. I'll be back in a week and test you on it. If you pass, you're in...part of my disciple band."

Absolutely not. Nothing of the kind.

Jesus already knew who they were. With His eyes He saw their hearts, and said simply, "Come. Come with me [and I will do something with your life]. I will make you fishers of men!"

The school they were going to was the school of life with Jesus. What He was offering was a life with Him. And in the powerful working of the Spirit that day, they knew that it was for them.

In the personal relationship with Jesus, He is interested in us. He listens to us. He invites us to tell Him our hearts. And He, with His healing hands, reaches out to us. It is a powerful offer of *acceptance*. The disciples needed it.

The men, and women, and young people of Rwanda and Burundi need it. It is an offer too wonderful to refuse. It is grace. It is not hard to see that something important, and potentially life-changing, is being offered them.

So the first message following the invitation to rest, is the offer of an intimate walk with Jesus.

The Claim of the Cross

The physical cross is not always there before them as they begin the retreat. Some, in the Pentecostal tradition, have been taught that symbols are not necessary, and that outward signs…indeed, all adornment…are unnecessary, if not an *offense*, to Jesus. So seeing a physical cross, we found, was a very direct challenge to some of those who had dared to come to the retreat.

In teaching, our colleague Tekle often traces the role and importance of blood in the sacrificial system of Israel. Blood represented sacrifice, the giving of oneself, the most precious thing one has to offer to God. So animal sacrifice became a very important part of Israel's worship, of its relationship with God. Abraham is ready to offer up his own son…a foretelling of what God Himself would do in Jesus.

So the concept of blood as giving of self, blood as cleansing, and blood as the open door to forgiveness, is explained at length. We are, after all, talking about Jesus Who took for Himself the role of the "Lamb of God, slain for the world."

Jesus is not offered simply as "ever lovin' friend," Who, in the modern American understanding, demands nothing and blesses everything. It is not love without roots, nor love without foundation, that is offered in these retreats.

What is offered is what the theologian Dietrich Bonhoffer of Germany called "The Nail-Torn God." What is held up for Rwanda, and the leaders of its Church, is not what Dietrich Bonhoffer called "cheap grace," but a love hard-bought, a love given through ultimate sacrifice through the excruciating pain of the lover.

What is offered is the One they already know, Who took our place in judgment, in execution, and in an ultimate penalty paid. This is not a picture of an absent God…a God who let history run away with His own plan, and defeat everything He had in His heart to do. Instead, it was the offer of God's own love, God's own life in HIS SON…in the darkest, most terrible day in history. It was a day in which even Jesus Himself felt abandoned and cried out, "My God, my God, why hast Thou forsaken me?" Yet He knew, as the great hymn assures us, that "standeth God within" the shadows, keeping watch above His own.

It is a powerful gesture for these church leaders of Central Africa. They know this God. They know this ultimate sacrifice of Christ. And they know the ways in which they…or others in their position…did not go all the way.

And yet, from the very cross, while the torture is happening and the world is doing its killing work, they hear again from the outstretched arms of Jesus Himself, while they are killing Him, crying, "Father, forgive them, for they know not what they do!" Forgiveness comes pouring from that hour of death…to save them.

The Gift of Forgiveness and the Cost of Unforgiveness

The retreat moves on to the theme of forgiveness, offered by the one on our team who has been trained as a teacher. This is the only time a blackboard is used.

Earnestly, compellingly, a picture is painted of the broken hearts of these wounded countries, those hurt leaders of the Church. The human heart is drawn on the board...then filled with little crosses...the picture of the hurts they've had, the wounds they've born. The logic is drawn out of what those hurts do to a person if they continue in the heart unredeemed, unforgiven. That is, they are passed on to other little hearts, the hearts of our children.

The cost of unforgiveness is made vivid by the picture of the lives of the Christian workers still wounded, bent over with the burden of those wounds...obviously unable, or only half able, to do the costly work of ministry.

But forgiven!...Daring to forgive what was done to them, and suddenly free! Suddenly upright! Suddenly able to go forward and serve as freed men, released prisoners, as people now able to look at others and their needs, and be able to serve them. Before forgiveness they were too bent with burdens to even see the needs of the world around them. It is a powerful teaching.

At that point, the offer is made to come to the cross. The physical cross has been introduced during the teaching on the cross. It stands now before them. Each one is essentially invited to tell his or her story.

"You are invited to tell the group, from your place in the circle, whatever there is pain in your life that you want to share, and when you are done, to come to the table in the center, and kneel before the Cross and let all of us, your brothers and sisters, gather around and lay hands on you and pray for your healing, your forgiveness, your freedom from the burden you have been carrying."

And so it begins...one and then another, no two exactly like the others, there "at the foot of the cross." There, in the first Rwanda retreat with these supposedly "unresponsive" Rwandan men, this process for twelve men went on for nearly eight hours. One man even went out to get a towel, to wipe the tears that had flooded there during that time.

Receiving those prayers...earnest, heartfelt prayers, largely offered by their own friends and fellow leaders with loving hands...is one of the high points of the retreat. Jesus *does* come, within this company of "the two or three gathered together," and He powerfully touches each one, and releases and frees them. The healing has already begun.

The Freeing Scriptures

These serious seekers, earnest and longing, and beginning to be so open in their own way, are not done when the shadows of afternoon lengthen. Unlike most Americans who go off to conferences and retreats, these people are perfectly willing, it turns out, to go on into the evening.

The retreat team itself is exhausted, and ready to rest. But these people have come to BE there. And, overwhelmed by the invitation of Jesus, they each receive two Scriptures as an assignment for that first night.

Particularly they take St. Paul's great passage to the Corinthians, in his second letter, the fifth chapter, where, in the seventeenth verse he describes what happens to a person when he or she receives Christ. That is, he becomes a new person, and He is given a new life. An exchange is made. His sins are poured into Christ and Christ's love, in the blood He shed for the world on the Cross, and it is poured into the sinner as wonderful forgiveness. And this becomes the message to be told to the world...the message of forgiveness. "For God was in Christ restoring (reconciling) the world to Himself." And we, Paul says, are ambassadors sent as reconcilers, to tell that message everywhere.

They gather in small groups. They pore over the passage. The next day, one from each group reports their findings. They have plumbed the depths. It turns out they have spent two or three hours turning the passage over and over, and looking at what it must mean for them.

"If we are ambassadors," they say, "then we represent someone else. We are not free to live for ourselves. We live for Jesus, and we represent Him." Their very telling of it next day is moving to us all. They are freed by the very truth of these wonderful words.

Either that night or the second night, the group is given the great passage from John 13, on the Last Supper, which of course is all about Jesus' washing His disciples' feet...a powerful teaching to them about humbling themselves in a ministry as servants. Making the point that if He, the Lord and Master, the great Rabbi, can wash *their* feet, then surely they can wash each others' feet, and the world's feet! We ask them to read it alone, personally, as a kind of individual meditation.

There is teaching on the Ministry of Love as the primary characteristic of God's heart toward the world, and of Jesus' ministry. His commandment to love, in the chapters of *John: 14-16*, are offered along with Paul's confirmation of the nature of love...the greatest gift...in *I Corinthians 13*.

Servant Ministry...and the Foot-Washing

The act of foot-washing is not practiced, for the most part, in the Rwandan Church...nor in the American Church. But this picture of servanthood, given by Jesus Himself, is inescapable as a key to the whole idea of the gathering at the table of those who love Jesus, as the power of that fellowship of friends. Elton Trueblood called this "The Incendiary Fellowship" of those who walk the way of love with Jesus.

It has been easy for the Church across the world to leave out, to ignore, this awkward practice...awkward most of all because it calls Christians, and particularly pastors, to bend the knee in humility before their people, before their colleagues, before God.

It became evident over time that the division and even hatred in these Great Lakes countries was not just between rival tribes. It was between rival churches as well. Deep feelings had come not only out of the turmoil of the genocide time, but out of the dominant position of one church both by numbers and by position vis á vis the government. Jealousy, hurt, and anger were all part of this divisiveness.

Now these people were coming to sit beside each other, on the same level, in a simple church, before the cross. And then, as the retreat drew toward its climax and close, they were led to a teaching that called them all to follow Jesus, to set aside all pretense to dignity, clerical power, and "place" above others, and to take on instead the humble role of a servant following Jesus.

It was a new idea. But it was there in Scripture, and it had been there from the beginning. It typified Jesus' own ministry.

Some leaders in the earliest retreats resisted it out of hand. Others, in later retreats, fought it within their own souls, even as the basins and towels and the Ethiopian and the old white man were approaching them round the circle.

It was as transforming as perhaps anything that was done during the retreats. All the teaching seemed to be gathered up in this act: They were being readied for a new ministry, with a new spirit.

The Lord's Supper at the Table Together

To come from that humbling experience, in which they sang and prayed and had their own feet washed, to the very simple offering of the bread, broken before them, and the wine poured out, and the great words spoken to and heard across the world, moved them all…moved all of us…by the Spirit's power, to a unity that could not have been manufactured, nor taught by precept. It was seen before them. It was demonstrated. The result was that they all knew, in each retreat that something had happened.

Evaluation

"What has this meant to you, to spend these three days, apart with Jesus?" we ask.

Their answers have been, over and over, like the young man of Burundi who had said the first day, "My brother was killed in the genocide. I know the murderer. I see him around the town. It is all I can do to keep from revenging."

But on the last day he said, "I want to go home…no, I am eager to go home. I want to find that man, and tell him that it is over between us. I forgive him."

Others, picking up on the Scripture they had so taken to heart, said:

> "I have a new name: RECONCILER!
> I have a new title: AMBASSADOR!
> I am of a new tribe: THE TRIBE OF JESUS!"

We linger as the parting time comes. Now there are smiles, and hugs, the holding of hands. There is begging that we return, and that the experience not stop, but have a chance to grow.

9

The Miracle Process and Power of Prayer

As we have journeyed out to the Great Lakes of Africa and gone finally to work in the deep things of the human heart, we have found our lives challenged, humbled, and subtly but deeply changed.

We have watched God work. We have seen Him do things in people's lives that none of us could have imagined, dreamed of, or planned…not even in our wildest and most grandiose moments.

That has been very humbling for me…to see such changes in the hearts of people.

Changes have come to me too. How could I *live*, much less function rationally and wholly, with any concern for others if *my* six children…including my tiny baby…had been murdered outside a church, particularly after the priest or pastor had refused entry for my family for protection and refuge there? Could I be leading a major church organization as my friend in Rwanda is trying to do? Would not I be a volatile person in danger of erupting in anger at the slightest provocation? Would I not find myself living sadly, with an overwhelming sense of loss and regret, complicated by a desire to fight back, to revenge those deaths?

How would I be calm and peaceful, a wise and patient leader? Perhaps four months after the first retreat, in a little prayer group of four of us, meeting as an exercise in the work of a later retreat, we found ourselves to have the chance to be quite candid with each other, and to let out our inner feelings. One of the people in the group of four of us was a young woman whose job...as a staff member of the Protestant Council of Rwanda...was to be the cleaning lady for their offices.

Quietly she described her life. She had several children at home, her husband had been killed in the genocide, and she was trying to carry on alone.

"Why, I didn't even know her before this retreat!" Immanuel exclaimed. "I didn't know about her life, so poor, and lonely." It seemed to soften his heart, encouraging him to say more.

"I have a problem that keeps overtaking me. It comes upon me when I least expect it. It erupts out of my heart and I say things I don't ever want to say. Things that hurt me...and others. It is a problem with anger."

He asked us to pray for him about that; and our little group did. His terrible loss had left him ravaged with grief, and had made it almost impossible for him to work or live peacefully with others. But there, in that setting of new trust, he was able to confess this overpowering torment in his heart.

Knowing of the grief and anger of this brother of mine from so far away, on the other side of the world, reminds me of the burdens of others. It reminds me of my own vulnerabilities, of my own hurts and angers. It calls me to the forgiveness of others, when I so often want them to ask forgiveness of me.

Awareness of my own vulnerability reminds me of how vulnerable we all are. My own pain, my own darkness, my own insecurities and fears become a means for my own reflection. They call me to greater kindness and greater care for all those around me.

The walls that grow up between us become so high, and feelings rise so easily. And we humans listen...all the time...to innuendo, to rumor, to hearsay. Stories are told us about other people...people we love, people with whom we work, people who are dear to us. And we tend to believe at least half of the lies, though usually they are not as others report to us. Barriers are built in human relationships. Vague feelings become confirmed truth in our minds. Afterwards we are wrong.

And, sooner or later, someone pays. Words are said. The misapprehensions are revealed. Hurt is done. We never intended it, but hurt is done.

Yet, people hate the walls. They hate the fear. They hate the talking about others, believing badly about others, and the feeling of disappointment about others.

They would far rather be one. They are much more thrilled, blessed, encouraged, given "a good feeling" by the experience of harmony of which the psalmist spoke: That it is like the anointing oil flowing down from Aaron's head, down his beard and robe to the hem of his garment. There is joy in that. There is fulfillment in that.

Something There is That Doesn't Like a Wall

Robert Frost is right. The forces of the world…no matter how many wall-building, negative ones there are…do not like walls. We do not like barriers. We do not like rules, traditions, barbed wire, or great gulfs that keep people out of where they have a right to be, or that keep them apart from those with whom they know they should be together with.

Jesus' most passionate prayer was "that they all may be one…as You, Father, are in me, and I in You."

God does not want His people divided. He does not want them at war. He wants "swords beaten into plowshares, and spears into pruning hooks." His vision through Isaiah was that He wanted the military academies down. He wanted the wars over. His picture was of the "peaceable Kingdom." He wanted the lion and the lamb lying down together.

"Peace I leave with you," He cried in John's Gospel. "I leave you peace not like the peace the world gives. But, a peace beyond human understanding."

The great desire of the heart of God is that His children...all the world's people, who all belong to Him...should be one family. This is why His whole work was to call them home to Him, to call them back from all those far-away places where they have gone in their hearts, away from God. Away from His love...away from the covenant, the bond they originally had with Him...as His children, given very life in the world by Him.

God's first intention, again, was to *reconcile* the world to Himself, to *restore* the world its Father, to its family life, to its unity of heart and spirit.

God's war is ever, and was always, against hate. Hating another is grievous sin with God; it was in the Commandments, it is in the teaching of Jesus who sends us into the world to bring about its healing, its restructure, its coming home. God's intention is...

Death to the Living with Hate

Unreconciled life was never God's intention for His own. His picture of the world He wanted, the world He created, the world He meant it to be...when He said, "Let there be light..." and "I will make man"...was that mankind would be like Him. And He did make man in His own image, the image of love. The image of Himself as One Who does love, as One who wants justice and fair play Who lives by mercy, and Whose way is compassion. He is not afraid to judge what is wrong, what is unlike Him, and what is unworthy of Him.

God puts in all of us the yearning to be one. This is found in the yearning of a man and a woman, in love, to be one with each other, and to have atonement made for every selfish thing, every unfair word that keeps them from each other.

There is an instinctive yearning of people to be one with other animals, and to tame the wild beast. They desire to come to an accommodation, a living together. When my dog, my companion of the mountain trails of summer, my fellow traveler in the car across the country, comes over by my chair in my study and lies down at my feet, he clearly is saying, "I want to be near you. You and your family are 'MY people.' I guard you. I protect you. I want to be with you. I love you."

The yearning to be one is instinctive. It is right. It is the God-given way to live. Everything that challenges that, and undercuts that, and perverts that, and works for separation, selfishness, and division is devilish and can come only from the Evil One.

The strange business of reconciliation is the central work of God for bringing people back into the reality, the healing and resting that makes life possible again for the world. It is the work that will endure. It is the new reality that alone can bring the new day of the lion and the lamb lying down together.

The Historic Way of the Church, Through Prayer and Scripture

God has called us to offer something very simple and very direct to this vast work of healing that is so needed by the hurt people of the Great Lakes region of Africa. It is so simple as to be almost ignored by the Church. Yet it comes directly out of the Church's own deepest experience, and it's highest heritage.

This is, quite simply, the heritage of prayer. Christians themselves rather glibly sometimes say, "I'll pray for you." Surely they mean to do it. But it is very tempting to forget this specific promise of prayer you've made. Yet, the intention is there, and despite human frailty, the Church of Christ through the ages has offered this unique gift to human society…the gift of the practice, power, and high tradition of prayer.

Jesus practiced prayer. He offered it as the very heart of His ministry. He healed the sick and raised the dead through the means of prayer. His disciples watched Him pray. That was part of what He would give them, part of the powerful teaching He would offer them as they accepted His invitation to "Come, follow Me."

They watched Him heal the sick that evening at the home of Peter's mother-in-law. They saw the demon cast out of the boy at the foot of the Mount of Transfiguration.

They finally asked Jesus to teach them to pray, as John had taught his disciples. And so came "The Lord's Prayer."

The company Jesus formed became notably marked as a praying company. They were to become a preaching company, for sure. But they would be more distinctive and more unique in all of human experience as a way, means, and power for living. This strange and wonderful thing they had learned to do is what the Church calls prayer.

They did not invent it. Jesus did not invent it. God the Father had given it to the family of man as the unique means of communication with Him: Adam and Eve talked with God in the Garden. Abraham heard God speak to him at his tent door on a starry night…when the promise came that he would be the father of many nations. Abraham prayed with Isaac at the moment of sacrifice. Joseph prayed as a prisoner in Egypt. Moses heard God's voice out of the flame of a burning bush, and his connection with God was perpetual as plagues mounted and the great Exodus came. The young Isaiah prayed in the temple in Jerusalem. David the King prayed passionately throughout his life. The whole heritage of Israel was a praying heritage, and Jesus made it a fine art. He practiced it as power, and He practiced it as love.

First the little band of disciples said, learned, and began to practice prayer, until it became, after Pentecost and its spirit of boldness from above, the daily means of the whole apostolic work. "Gold and silver have I none," cried Peter to the lame beggar at the beautiful gate of the temple that afternoon in Jerusalem, "but such as I have I give you. In the Name of Jesus Christ of Nazareth, rise up and walk!" And into the temple the man went "walking, and leaping, and praising God," just as others had done at the hand of Jesus.

Prayer was the unique mark of the early Church's life. Not only did Peter, Paul, and the twelve pray, but the whole Church prayed. At a prayer meeting, in the face of persecution, the whole building where they were gathered shook at the prayers of the apostolic company together. At Pentecost, not even language held them back. They spoke that day in the tongues of all the many people gathered in Jerusalem. They knew the *Power* had come...the power of the Spirit of God. It was the Holy Spirit, the very breath of God Himself.

In that breath...just as Jesus had said in the Upper Room after the Resurrection, "Receive the Holy Spirit," and later, "Do not leave the city until you have received power from on high"...a strange power belonged to the Church that was recognized and used in varying degrees and ways, by the most ordinary of the Church's people throughout the ages. The early saints and bishops prayed. The martyrs prayed. The reformers prayed. Monks and evangelists prayed. The people gathered in congregations prayed.

Perhaps only with the rise of modern science, and particularly with the advent of modern medicine, did it begin to seem less important to pray. There seemed to be emerging, in the 18th century, other kinds of power to heal the sick and help human lives. With the rise of this new medicine and the self-centeredness of the Enlightenment, many suspected that God was not needed at all.

And the Church of the West, at least, grew almost afraid of prayer, other than in its most formal, congregational use. The "mainline" churches of America in the mid-20th century, in their passion to "do justly, and love mercy, and walk humbly with God," put their emphasis more and more on actions that could be taken, almost literally, to "bring in the kingdom." Prayer came to seem more and more mystical to them, if not even a little threatening, especially as other needs of the Church and theological speculation began to lay claim to prayer's power, and especially its power to heal the sick.

At that very time a modern healing movement began to grow. Agnes Sanford and Francis McNutt were among mid-century teachers of the reality of prayer. Oral Roberts and others brought prayer to the television airwaves.

As the century came to a close, a movement known as "healing touch" mounted across a wide, diverse spectrum, and began to be taught to nurses in New York's Mount Sinai Hospital. The Alcoholics Anonymous movement realized prayer's quiet power to heal the brokenness of spirit in alcoholism. Public television's Bill Moyer dared to do a series on the many known forces of healing, from "alternative medicine" forms to the long-known laying on of hands, as the followers of Jesus have proclaimed it.

The Church of Africa, India, South America, and Indonesia seems never to have lost prayer's power. Huge churches have grown in South Korea centered on the daily practice of prayer…with staggering numbers going apart to "prayer mountains" for early morning prayer.

The African Church has always had a high sense of the spirit world, and the power of the spiritual in human life. The need of the world, of America, and surely, of the Great Lakes countries of Africa, is to recover that very power.

As the Rwandan and Burundian churches struggle to recover from their own failures in the genocide time, many outsiders have come with help to heal broken hearts. Most credible seemed at first to be the understandings of the trauma produced by horrific violence. These were largely psychological approaches. Analyses were offered, and techniques were put forth. Principles were outlined to help the understanding of church leaders and others who wanted to help.

There seemed to be the assumption that if you learned the causes and the observable phenomena, you would somehow be able to <u>be</u> healed, and bring it about in others. As if understanding was the first step toward solution…as in many situations it can be.

But the cry coming to our little team, as we took simply prayer, and the work of healing that came directly from the *Bible*, was "We need to be healed ourselves. It is not just knowing *about* trauma that we need, it is healing for our own souls, so that we, with strength, can reach out to heal others."

These simple things of Scripture, prayer, testimony, and of the offer of love, seemed so obvious and pious as to be overlooked...even by the Church. Yet, they were immediately recognized by those Church leaders who had been through the understanding stages, but who had come to see that something needed to happen to their own hearts. *They themselves needed healing.*

It is this experimenting and practice which appears to be a contribution this ministry from middle America can offer. It is a kind of reminder to the Rwandan Church of what it always knew...of the very things with which its pastors are most familiar as those truths and values dearest to them all. Here they could see a way to apply what they knew, believed, and brought to bear...for their own needs, and for the needs of their own churches and communities...and, indeed, throughout their entire countries.

Giving Hope

"If you had come with this message, and these healing retreats of prayer right after the genocide," one leader of a major evangelical church group told us in early 1997, "Rwanda would be two-thirds of the way toward being healed by now."

It is probable that the task is much larger, and would have taken much longer, and that it still will. But the healing retreats have opened the way for some quite clear signs of hope in both these countries.

As we began our retreats and recorded the first encouraging responses, often with testimonies of deep personal healing in the lives of the participants, it was evident that:

> Here was something every pastor could do. Every Christian lay leader also knew something about all aspects of the retreat assumptions. Its power for them was based on experience of something happening to them in the course of the retreat.
> They were healed as they were prayed for by others.

"Reconciliation" was a fundamental thrust of God Himself into the world, and it was the first and most basic reach of God toward His children.

They learned it is possible to forgive a person even before that person has ever said, "Sorry." It was Jesus Himself Who, directly from the cross, while the world was killing Him, said, "Father, forgive them, for they know not what they do." Jesus suddenly became the great model to them of a breakthrough in the process of finding mending for their lands.

They learned to rest in Jesus.

They learned to be with Jesus...to hear His heart and His teaching.

They learned the awesome power of His sacrifice of His shedding blood for them. They found that it was cleansing. It was a new life...new blood...for them.

They were challenged to see Jesus on His knees, washing His followers' feet and calling them to Servant Ministry. They saw a new way that the life of the Table, the supper of love could draw them into unity with each other.

Suddenly there was the means before them for not only breaking down walls between Tutsi and Hutu, but between Protestant and Catholic, between Pentecostal and Anglican. Maybe even more profoundly, there was a means for breaking down walls between the "LIONS" of the church...the "big men," bishops, and "legal representatives"...and the people of the churches. For here was deep division.

Suddenly there is hope that all barriers can be broken. That Jesus is not blocked by any wall if He, in His sacrificing love, can be claimed, and received, and taken in as new source of power. Love emerges as a reality that is far deeper than the seductive relationships with the people of power, especially government power that had been so tempting to church leaders before the genocide.

Various clerical powers are always a temptation in the Church anywhere in the world. The call to Servant Ministry, symbolized in the washing of feet, becomes a visible sign of a call back to the very style and spirit of Jesus' own ministry, and the ministry He left for His followers forever.

Changed Lives Before Us

Leaders have found their own ways of taking back into their worlds the things they've learned from the reconciliation retreats. We had previously thought the means of expansion and reaching throughout the countries would be to hold more retreats.

However, soon a variety of responses were being made. In Burundi, in addition to retreats, Bible studies with the theme of reconciliation began, and a reconciliation conference for business leaders was held in a hotel. A youth crusade with the theme of reconciliation took place. Soon came the gathering of a national committee of leaders from across the denominational spectrum. This has become a new central focus for future approaches, with denominational barriers slowly, but surely, being broken down. A new unity is already coming.

A crusade in Burundi's Gitega…on the theme of reconciliation…brought 10,000 people to the city square, some sitting in trees to hear what was to them a new message. "Where have you been hiding this wonderful message?" the organizers asked our Tekle who had preached there.

Close to Bujumbura, a pastor who had refused to attend a Pilgrim Center retreat because he had been to seminars and workshops and felt they had not made any difference, sent his wife and an assistant as representatives to one of our retreats. Those two were so changed upon returning home that the pastor came to the next retreat…and then suddenly insisted on organizing a crusade in his community! Both there and in Gitega, pastors and their people were humbled and actually kneeled or stretched out on the ground, praying, confessing, repenting, crying, and opening their hearts to the new power God had for them.

One life after another was changed before us. "I am no longer afraid," one pastor said. "I am free! I am free!" said another, so touched in retreat by the message of reconciliation.

God's Work Through Open Hearts

We believe an awesome work of God is being done, merely through hearts open to His leading and His love. It is being done through very ordinary people, and His working in and upon people who are willing to be touched.

The Christian leaders of Rwanda and Burundi know that horrible things happened in their land. They have known since the genocide that deep changes still must happen in their countries. At the beginning it seemed that programs, printed material, food and medicine, and perhaps new organizations…even new churches with new names…might make the difference.

It seems clearer now that knowing the right answers is not enough. Something still needs to change, and it is more and more evident that change needs to come in the human heart. And to change the heart is to work deep into the soul, so that change can come in the very being of the person.

Many coming to our small three-day retreat come with real hope. Though they are often wary, there is a readiness to have something happen to them. They believe in God. They know He can do something in and for them. The readiness factor is real.

The team itself has learned that change in people will not come by virtue of some skill we have, nor by some vast knowledge or expertise we bring to the retreats. The message to the retreatants as we gather is: "We are not experts. We do not come out of any great knowledge. We come as people of the World Church who care about you. We come in love on their behalf. We come to be with you…to stand with you. To be on your side."

The message goes on to say, "We believe the agenda for the retreat is the Holy Spirit's agenda. We are here to follow Him in His leading."

We too, are affected by what the Spirit does in these gatherings. We feel as a team that we are there to take God seriously, and to take the Bible and all it offers seriously.

It is a very simple approach. It is in fact, a pious approach. It emphasizes the simplest things of Scripture and truth. We do not want to be known for our knowledge, our degrees, or our expertise. We do want to be known for the results...for what happens, and what really takes place in these times together. Truly, something *has* happened. With every person something happens. We can see it, and they tell us. God's work is being done...through open hearts.

It has become more and more clear to us that we have not been given the whole work. Trauma specialists have come, psychiatrists and social workers have come. Many teach, and understanding grows.

Much of what others do we could not do. We are not trained to do it. Every approach makes an important contribution. Ours is a niche business, plain and simple. It is a small...but crucial...piece that we have been given.

The Late Life Call

To us the marvel is that this call came after it seemed our work was over and done...after forty years of parish ministry, and a time when many "retire," has been humbling and amazing. This call to Molly...to a ministry at which she is very good, and which she loves...was certainly not planned by either of us.

But friends said, "We want you to have a ministry. We do not want this to be the end." They raised funds to create what first became the Rouner Center for Mission and Ministry, and then, over time, The Rouner Center for Reconciliation.

It has given us a new life, and we are changed. Like the young people of Burundi, we too, have a new name: Reconciler. We now have our new title: Ambassador. We too, are of the new tribe, the world tribe: *The tribe of Jesus.* It is God's work...His wonderful healing, pure and simple.

10

New Lives of Mission: "See...I'm Doing a New Thing!"

Tekle has gone to our World Vision partners to tell the stories of what is happening as Rwanda and Burundi have responded to the reconciliation theme in the work that God has given us among them:

> Pastors and others are on their hands and knees weeping in repentance and asking forgiveness, praying anew for reconciliation. Ten thousand people have gathered for those meetings in Gitega's city square.
>
> Another pastor was at first resistant to anything more on reconciliation. He'd given up, but he now sees results. He came to one retreat, and organized a crusade in his Bujumbura suburb, which gathered two thousand. His own church has changed to a mixture of both Hutu and Tutsi, of working people and government and community leaders.
>
> Formerly resistant churchmen at both ends of the denominational spectrum, came together to form a Burundi National Committee for Reconciliation. The Pilgrim Center works through them now. Anglican bishops are there. Catholic bishops and Pentecostal legal representatives have come. What the Church in Burundi dreamed of is now happening, as the church leaders' "Forum" has gathered for weekly Wednesday breakfast gatherings.
>
> World Vision Burundi and Burundi's Church called for reconciliation retreats for every month. In August, 1998, it began to hap-

pen. Two retreats happened in Burundi…led by people the Pilgrim Center has trained. These local people took the initiative.

Africa Revival Mission in Rwanda held a reconciliation retreat, following the Pilgrim Center model. It is the way change comes for them and in them.

In Kenya, what was once a young Pokot's dream…i.e., reconciliation along his country's border with Uganda…has begun to happen with support and leadership from the Pilgrim Center. In June, 1998, the first Pokot/Karamoja meeting was held in Kitale. By June's end another was held at World Vision in Kenya. Government officers from Uganda and Kenya came. Four tribes became involved, and the Pilgrim Center team joined them for a third meeting in Kampala in early November. World Vision Kenya and Uganda saw its importance and asked for additional support for this work.

Following the bombing along the border of Ethiopia and Eritrea, the government asked church leaders of both countries to meet to work toward reconciliation. The Pilgrim Center supported the meeting, and our Center's Ethiopian program director was invited to lead an ensuing meeting in Nairobi.

Invitations came from two towns in Congo, begging for reconciliation retreats to be held. World Vision said, "We're surprised." They had commissioned the joint venture, but they've been surprised. It is becoming more clear that it is God's work and that *He* is doing something new. He is surprising the professionals! Something outside of their plans, procedures, and expectations is happening.

Curiously, it seems to be something new. God is doing something through a new approach…a new, disarming undertaking. Perhaps this quixotic enterprise is an emerging model for one of many new ways God wants to do mission in this new day, new century, new millennium. It appears to involve a daring willingness to go, ordinary people being used in new ways, a centering on the healing work of love, the surrounding support of business and professional people who had never thought of themselves as missionaries, and the creation of new definitions of mission.

People Seeking Significance Beyond Success

A growing number of younger people have come forward in the last two decades of the 20th century, saying, "I want to go to Africa. I've seen the pictures. I've heard the stories. I've seen the lives of friends who've gone. I want what they have. I want to see what they've seen. I am ready to have 'my heart broken by the things that break the heart of God.'"

They almost come out of the woodwork, asking for a way to be involved. They come because they have begun to recognize something in their lives very like the picture painted by Bob Buford in his book about going *From Success to Significance*.

Many of these young people are successful. They have successful businesses and have made money far beyond any reasonable expectation. They are in the clubs. They have friends. They all recognize it. They have, in a few cases, become prominent in their churches…as leaders, as givers.

But secretly they ask, "Is there not something more? Something I can do, something I can be, that is different from my success? Could I have an influence, make a difference in ways that are far beyond the products I can produce, the capital I can make?"

Some of them, because of a friend's leadership, have gone to Africa. They have come back to search their souls, to look at their lives and ask, "How could it be different?"

One young lawyer said, "Not a day passes that I do not think of Africa." It has caused him to look differently at his money. He talks with business friends about a concept of "Kingdom Oil"…of investing resources in ministries and movements that are changing the city. He heads a foundation that has begun eagerly to fund their enterprises of faith.

Another set out to make every Friday a day of retreat, of *Bible* study, of prayer.

Many of them have helped to build Windpumps in Africa so that water can be more accessible to tribal people living close to the edge in northwest Kenya.

Some have moved into entire new jobs that fit more closely with their new understandings of the world.

The Role of Missions in Giving New Meaning to Late Life

There is a view in American society, largely shared by Christians in the land, that the goal of long working lives is to rest at the end. Saving for retirement is the task, preparing to have a life largely of recreation after your working days are done.

When a family member of the next generation challenged 70-year-old Molly, saying, "Why don't you just go to Mexico instead of to Africa, and lie on a beach in the sun?" Molly's answer came back, quick as a shot: "That's not the way I choose to live my life!"

We had imagined at one time, buying a house on the Wisconsin bluffs above the St. Croix River and working our way into a life of watching the river, and remembering the years of service. It has not worked out that way. Mission has entirely changed our perceptions of life. The years to and from Africa, and the opportunity, right at the point of leaving parish life, of making extended journeys to Africa, to serve a calling higher than anything we had ever known before, changed all that.

No one had ever offered us this life as part of a "retirement plan." No one had said, "Now, where around His world would you like to serve?"

We knew there was Peace Corps for older people....President Carter's mid-70's mother had been a wonderful example of that. Perhaps she set the pace. Following her were the unexpectedly retired President of the United States, her son, and his wife Rosalyn, after suddenly bolting up in bed one night and saying, "I've got it! International conflict resolution!"

It is what he had done skillfully and boldly as President. He would do it again. The world needed it more than ever, and he and she are doing it...in Ethiopia, Haiti, and Bosnia.

That is not all he does. He serves out in the world, and the media began to dub him, "Our most successful Ex-President." There is greatness about service. Others have seen it and found it compelling as an example.

"Mission"...serving others in the cause of caring for human need, going to the world in the Name of Jesus, pouring yourself out for the interests of others...whether it is building Habitat for Humanity houses, or ending the scourge of hunger, is a vital center, framework, and context for the very living of late life.

Mission is peculiarly, about movement, about changes, about people going to people, and meeting in the most elementary human way. It is not about dominance. It is not about over-powering. It is about being *beside* other people. It is about "getting to know you," as the song says.

In some ways mission demands slowing down, and looking carefully, and listening carefully, to another. This is something particularly difficult for Americans in this century, in a time when the emphasis on communication in the form of information, conversation, and reporting is done *fast*. We say things quickly. We even use, if possible, abbreviations in speech, so we can talk faster.

Implied in that goal is being *done* with it. It is saying it and doing it quickly, and then getting on, getting out of there. There is a certain unspoken impatience, a sort of hurry.

This pressure hurries relationships. It cuts them short. It even prevents relationships by not allowing time to look in the other's eyes, to sense the other's spirit by what his or her face and body are saying, as well as by what their words are saying.

It is peculiar to the "Two-Thirds World," that it takes time in relationships. It knows the quality of taking time, of listening, or responding...and so, goes deeper to the heart. One is more likely in these settings to *know* the heart…even when translation is necessary. Americans so easily lose the relationship, the meaning, because we are in a hurry to say it and be gone.

It may be that age is more amenable to the things that make for mission: The coming together of people, the quiet conversation, the listening that makes way for loving. When love has a chance to operate, the delivery of its message…the Good News which the missionary bears…is more likely to take into account what has been discovered about the other person, what is seen to be the spirit and heart and need of the other person.

Mission both gives meaning and purpose to the life of the older person, who has lived, learned, and gathered experience and wisdom, and who is ready to give it back, making use of a quality of patience that may make the communicating and the truth-telling more easily heard. This is something God can use in new ways, for great good.

New Kinds of Mission

Subtly, a change appears to have come for the American Church in its understanding of "mission".

Local congregations want to do "mission" themselves. In one decade, the idea of a layperson actually venturing out to be a missionary, albeit for a short time, is no longer new. It is not strange. It is being done…extending out across the world, as small "teams" of people, accompanied or not by their pastors, journeying to another part of their own country, or, more likely to a far country characterized by its great poverty. Many teams go to help build something…a building, possibly a school or clinic, or a gathering place of some kind in the midst of a vital mission in Mexico, Haiti, or even further away in Central or South America. Even going to Africa, India, or the Philippines is no longer uncommon.

This going-out does not replace what a full-time, long-term missionary committed to serving for a lifetime in one place can do. But there is an important place for ordinary Christians to go to other countries to stand beside and encourage and love and bring resources to bear from the West. The Western Church still has a profound obligation and call to care about the world...indeed, to "be" out there, across the world.

And, the going is happening. "Mission trips" for high school-aged church young people have become a compelling part of the growing-up of young Christians in the late decades of the 20th Century. What is also happening is the coming-to America, and to other countries of the West, of Christian leaders from the countries that first received Western missionaries.

"Third World" theological teachers came to occupy temporary chairs in American theological institutions. African, Indian, Chinese, and Southeast Asian pastors and evangelists came on tours, visiting churches and individuals who had helped them. They brought a message...a refreshing, stirring, renewing message...directly out of the experiences of the young churches of their countries. Their experience is elemental, biblical, Spirit-filled. It speaks simple faith. It expresses joy. It is marked by song and dance.

The character of the lives of these Christian leaders and their people often is marked by simplicity, by utter believing, and by deep commitment. Christianity is "serious business."

Mission has always meant travel. But it has become back-and-forth travel. Ordinary people go to places that tourists never go, and they sit down with ordinary people thousands of miles away, and they become friends.

The American churches are much less eager to support denominational strategies of mission...which often are held over from an earlier day and generation. Instead of sending obligatory money off to the denominations to spend it...on someone else going to be the missionary...the congregations have grown into a whole new interest themselves. They will raise and give far more money than before, but they want their own people to go and see, to hear the experiences, to be the missionaries...going to those in need.

The home church is soon willing to hear of the need...partly because their own fellow churchmen have gone and returned with the stories of their own transforming experiences. And so others see the transformation in the person, and hear the compelling message, and want to go themselves across that great gulf, from Middle America to the heart of Africa.

It is a going time...a traveling time. The network and the family grows, of connected men and women across the world.

These people from home go to the world and meet people. They become friends. They correspond. Ties are bound. Bonds are forged. The world...through Christian community...comes home.

A New Witness of Presence

"Presence" has always been powerful. It is personal. It is flesh and blood. It is being there. Even in our "high tech" day there are those wise enough to say that at the same time, we need to be "high touch." We invite people to go with us, to be trained into our healing ministry work, and we ourselves begin to realize that what is working is that there are gifts of reaching out that God has given our team...very subtle, very instinctive gifts. As Tekle says, "It is all in the heart. The heart that instinctively reaches out, as opposed to the heart that seems closed, that calls upon others to do the reaching out.

Of course, those with whom we work, in Rwanda and Burundi, are so wounded to begin with, and in many cases they are apprehensive and suspicious of us. We need to be very sure that all of us, as a team, are <u>able</u> to do the original, instinctive, reaching out to them.

People mean so much. Their "persons," their personalities, mean so much. It must always have been so.

Paul, the first great missionary of the Church, had to have been a compelling person, a presence...of whatever size or look...that commanded attention. People knew he was there. There was a passion about him, a fire in his soul, that made him a persistent and persuasive communicator.

Peter was described as "bold" in his apostolic preaching.

Philip, going down the Gaza Strip, ever at the ready as the Ethiopian prince came along, was not a nobody.

Andrew, fabled to have journeyed with the Gospel all the way to Cape Cormorant at the tip of India, could hardly have been a nonentity.

Patrick, and Columba, and the other Augustine missionary to Britain in a later day, were brave and bold people, with a spirit like that emblazoned on Patrick's breastplate, "I bind unto myself today, the strong Name of the Trinity!"

John Wesley, off on his horse to preach in the fields of England to 10,000 people at a time, E. Stanley Jones, off to India in another century, and Frank Laubach to the Philippines, were missionary statesmen. No one could say they were "the bland leading the blind."

Yet, in a day when the American missionary tradition of the 20th century seems to have stepped back from the going, in favor of technical and other supports for proclamation in "the field," and even feeling that "the day of missions is over," there is growing a new conviction that you have to go. As Bob Dylan sings, "You've got to serve somebody!" There is nothing quite like going yourself, and not only "being there," but offering yourself there.

It was a telling revelation when Jean Pierre of Burundi wrote, "You embraced us, with a pure clean love." His heart recognized a kindred heart.

Such "presence" as little teams of lay people go winging off across the world…just to be there with the people of need…is perhaps a new kind of witness, or maybe an old way of witnessing, just right for a new day. We hope and pray our healing work is an example of such a witness.

Translators and Transformation

The work of our team from Middle America is dependent upon translators and translation. How we wish it were not so. Even Tekle, the

African, needs translation in Rwanda and Burundi. Molly and I have studied a little French, but none of us speak Kirundi.

Yet, God blesses our efforts. He uses our eyes, our voices, our hands, the "English" of our bodies, to communicate…even deeply. But all the while, our work is done, the retreats are conducted, and our personal relations are carried on, through translation and translators.

They *emerge* in the retreats. And though we have found fine translators, often others come to the fore and simply step in and help. They pass it back and forth, and they enter into the spirit of the message as the teaching is being given.

What we have discovered is a kind of spiritual counterpoint that takes place. Rather than having translation and the need for a third person as a go-between being a barrier, what transpires is a kind of work of the Spirit, where the translator adds something of his or her faith to the process…a kind of movement, and joy, and eagerness.

At the same time, the translations slow down the process of communication, giving time for us to think not only of the next words, but to see the response and to more carefully sense how we are being received. This whole work, resulting from the slow, intense communication, is a work of transformation of fears being set aside, of resistance being disarmed, and of something new happening in the heart.

Through this means, which could be awkward but isn't, we see people opening up to us…as friends, and to God as the One alone Who can heal their hearts. It has unfolded as a miracle process to us.

Mission Lifestyle

I loved the life of parish ministry. I loved the regularity of it, the deep involvement with people's lives, the privilege…invited and sought…of presence at the highest and most hurting moments in the lives of individuals and families. I loved doing weddings and funerals. I loved going as pastor to hospital bedsides and to homes of need. I loved ministry with the young as they prepared for Church membership. I loved taking people on "Journeys of the Heart" and being an instrument for God's change in their lives. I loved preaching and teaching...the great honor of the pulpit...and the privilege of being able to address the issues of the day in the light of the Gospel...telling truth, proclaiming love, and helping people as I could, to understand the work of God in the life of our time.

But God has given me something new...a "second career," if you will. But it is far more that! It is a life with different assumptions, a different pace, and a different purpose.

In some ways the pace is slower. I no longer work the eighty and ninety-hour weeks that were common for me as a parish minister for at least the last 32 of my 40 years in the ministry. I am not answerable to 3,800 people. I do not have to guide and care for and direct a staff of forty, ten of them professional ministry people. I no longer need to attend church council meetings, or sit with committees and labor with them toward strategies and plans for future work.

Yes, we have a staff, but it is very small. We very much work as comrades, as a family. Our total work is mission. It all is directed at going out. Our image, our logo, our ethos, our purpose is "Journey Out." It is pilgrimage. It is moving out across the world...as one...to serve.

By God's grace and direction, I have left BIG behind: Big pulpit, big congregation, big budget, and big buildings...and always big responsibility. It is a new ministry in the "house by the side of the road," where I often had dreamed, with the poet, of being where I can "be a friend to man."

It is a slower ministry, a quiet ministry. It is a focused ministry...on healing the heart, on listening to the soul...whether at Starbucks in Edina over a cup of coffee, or in a circle of the "wounded healers" of the genocide lands of Rwanda and Burundi. Or heading west to the Cheyenne River Reservation in South Dakota, to be with our Indian comrades who lead little churches there. Or even going on the air to talk sense and speak peace to the people of Minnesota on all there really is to life, on what's important, on who God is, and who they are.

It is a style of life. It isn't retirement. It isn't golf or tennis. It is a life with a new balance...between journeying out across the world to serve, and time at home with family and a quiet friendship ministry of presence. It is possibly, a new "style" of mission. At least it is a new lifestyle for this couple who have heard and are trying to heed a call to a great new life "out there" beyond the bonds of parish life that were our discipline and our delight for full forty years.

Whatever that life is, its core and center is mission. It is the risk and expense of going out...beyond our "comfort zone," as one of our young business Africa travelers is wont to say.

It is going with angels sent before us to take us safely to the place God has prepared for us, as He promises in *Exodus 23:20*. It is a life of being constantly cast upon God, feeling our every move utterly dependent on Him. In that is great joy.

New Life in Old Age

"Never say old," many have said to us as I have somewhat joked about what we are doing in our old age.

Plainly we are old by America's formal working standards. The advantage is that at 65 we become pensioners and do not need to have a job that pays. We can give ourselves to ministry wherever it leads us.

Of course, the huge generosity of Christian brothers and sisters who provided a corpus of funds at the end of the 32-year Colonial Church ministry, have entirely made possible the existence of The Pilgrim Center for Reconciliation. We fly to the world and work in far places and lead "journeys out" because those people loved us and wanted us to have a ministry "post-parish."

God has done that, and wonderfully, He has done the rest. Our many plans, meetings, and projections have all helped. But these years have been all God's. None of what has happened was, nor could have been, foreseen.

Friends across the globe have come as gift upon gift. Growing credibility, quietly fought for as we have determined to stick with our work, and our Biblical faith and prayer concept of retreat for reconciliation work, has come "slowly by slowly," without ever asking. Again, this has been a gift.

And now suddenly, we are not only leading retreats with church leaders in Rwanda and Burundi, but we are initiating peace meetings between warring groups like the Pokot of Kenya and the Karamoja of Uganda. Even Eritrean church leaders have turned to us to help support and even give leadership to their attempts at meeting across the lines of war with their counterparts in Ethiopia.

It is, for Molly and me, and for Tekle too, a starting over, a second career. It is something new.

Seeing Life Anew

We did not design this life. It was simply given to us, but we know grace when it comes. And He has helped us to see all of life ANEW.

As we are born again into new life with Christ, we're also born into a new life of service that is not parish ministry. It is service that is more than the parish. It is more even than preaching, and the joy and wonder of hushed Christmas crowds and overflowing Easter audiences.

It is simple ministry. Slow ministry. Maybe lonely ministry. Certainly it is traveling ministry. Of course, it is risk ministry. It is attempting something so impossible that only God can bring it to pass and help it flourish.

All of life we see as new. Our grandchildren see something new in us, in the way we are loving life. They know it is outward. It is serving. It is there as witness to all who know us.

We believe they see the joy in it...and the challenge, the risk. It could be over tomorrow...for both of us, together. Land mines do go off. Guerrillas do attack. Accidents do happen. It could be over in a minute.

We pray for years to serve, and perhaps later, to reflect.

New Call, New Claims, New Energy, New Purpose

The call from God is a new one. It is a Macedonian call to "come over and help us." The claim upon us is from Jesus, our Lord, and it is real. It involves our hearts, our energy, our time, and our money.

It is a challenge to our faith…which needs to keep growing or we die. Our purpose is also new…but it grew out of the Gospel purpose of all the years past.

For us, there is joy even in the newness, and even in the different style, the different pace. We exercise. We see our grandchildren. We welcome our children. We take time for friends. We drink coffee. We board airplanes…again, and again, and again.

We follow God…into the years, however many or few, lie ahead. It is a wonder beyond any expectation that was our own. It is all good, this "New Life of Mission." If it carries a message to others…to come along, and journey out with us…so much the better.

We are privileged to stand among the peacemakers, people of the great Mennonite and Quaker peace-making history who have born a faithful witness for generations, and who have been blessed. We are privileged to watch healing happen and little parts of our world being reconciled.

It is in Other Hands. That is all that matters.

About the Author

Arthur Rouner grew up in a parsonage in Portsmouth, New Hampshire. He married Molly Safford in 1950. They have six children and five grandchildren. From 1954 to 1959, Dr. Rouner served as Minister of the First Congregational Church of Williamsburg, Massachusetts; from 1959 to 1962, The Eliot Church of Newton, Massachusetts, and from 1962 to 1994, The Colonial Church of Edina, Minnesota. In 1994, he founded The Pilgrim Center for Reconciliation.

Since 1982, Dr. Rouner has made many journeys annually to Africa to help with famine relief, water resources, and orphans, and currently, with reconciliation and peace-making efforts in Rwanda, Burundi, Congo, Kenya, and Uganda. He leads American volunteers on journeys of mission and personal transformation to Kenya, Ethiopia, and Uganda, and leads volunteer teams to encourage church leaders and congregations of the Cheyenne River and Cass Lake Indian Reservations.

Among his honors have been being named as "Best Minister in the Twin Cities," one of the "Ten Most Influential Ministers in the Twin Cities," one of the "100 Most Influential People of Minnesota," and "Clergyman of the Year." He is the author of fourteen additional books on the topics of reconciliation, Congregational Church history, practical ecumenism, the life of prayer and healing, the issues of love and marriage, human sexuality, the doctrine and work of the Holy Spirit, the faith foundations of the American nation, and the whole work of pastoral ministry.

0-595-23906-4